# HISTORY IN CLOSE-UP

## THE MEDIEVAL WORLD

COLOURPOINT
EDUCATIONAL

Sheila Turner Johnston
Norman Johnston

First Edition
Third Impression, 2017

ISBN: 978 1 904242 96 3

Layout and design: April Sky Design
Printed by: W&G Baird Ltd, Antrim

**Colourpoint Educational**
*An imprint of Colourpoint Creative Ltd*
Colourpoint House
Jubilee Business Park
21 Jubilee Road Newtownards
County Down
Northern Ireland
BT23 4YH

Tel: 028 9182 0505
Fax: 028 9182 1900
E-mail: sales@colourpoint.co.uk
Web site: www.colourpointeducational.com

## About The Authors

**Sheila Turner Johnston** had a career in both public and educational librarianship before jointly setting up Colourpoint Books in 1993. She has now retired although she continues to write. She is the joint author of the Foundation level edition of *Peace, War and Neutrality – Britain, Northern Ireland and Eire 1931–49* and *The Middle Ages* and author of *History in Close-Up: The Twentieth Century* published in 2010 and *Alice: A life of Alice Milligan*, published in 1994. She has won prizes for both fiction and non-fiction and has published many short stories. Her first novel, *Maker of Footprints*, was published by Plover Fiction in 2008.

**Norman Johnston** had many years experience of teaching History and of involvement in curriculum development. He was Head of History at Omagh Academy, Co Tyrone, 1980-96 and Moderator for GCSE History Coursework in Northern Ireland 1991-7. With Sheila Johnston, he founded Colourpoint Books in 1993. He was the author of *The Norman Impact on the Medieval World*, much of which is incorporated in this book, and *Peace, War and Neutrality – Britain, Northern Ireland and Eire 1931–49* (both by Colourpoint). He has also written many books on transport subjects. Norman sadly passed away in 2014.

# CONTENTS

# ICONS USED IN THIS BOOK

## GUIDE TO ICONS

 ACTIVITY

 BEFORE YOU START

 BY THE WAY

 PROJECT

 RESEARCH

 REVIEW

 TIP

 WORD BOX

 WRITER INFO

QUESTIONS

## SKILLS AND CAPABILITIES KEY

COMMUNICATION

MATHS

USING ICT

MANAGING INFORMATION

THINKING, PROBLEM SOLVING, DECISION MAKING

BEING CREATIVE

WORKING WITH OTHERS

SELF MANAGEMENT

# INTRODUCTION
# UNIT 1: DATES AND CENTURIES

History isn't all about dates, but to understand when things happened and to be able to sort out what happened before or after something else happened, you do need to understand dates and centuries.

Dates and centuries are really easy to work out when you get used to it. Look at these years:

2008 was in the 21st century

1572 was in the 16th century

204 was in the 3rd century

1836 was in the 19th century

Do you see a pattern in these dates and their centuries? What is it?

There are 100 years in a century. In the diagram below, each box represents a century.

| **1 – 100** | **101 – 200** | **201 – 300** | **301 – 400** |
|---|---|---|---|

What was the last year in the 1st century?

What was the first year in the 2nd century?

What was the first year in the 21st century?

So years that end in '00' are in the previous century! For example, **1300** was in the **13th** century, but **1301** was the first year of the **14th** century.

*'AD' is put before (or after) dates **after** the birth of Jesus. It is short for **'Anno Domini'**, which is Latin for 'The year of our Lord'.*

*'BC' is put after dates before the birth of Jesus. It is short for **'Before Christ'.***

*So the year AD1000 was one thousand years after Jesus' birth.*

*Actually, early calendars may have got it a bit wrong. Scholars think that Jesus may have been born between three and five years BC!*

*Sometimes you will see the terms **'CE'** and **'BCE'** used instead. They refer to the same times but stand for **'Current Era'** and **'Before Current Era'**.*

1. Name a date in the 18th century.
2. In which century was AD1900?
3. Name a date in the 5th century.
4. In which century was AD1235?

When we talk about years that are BC, we have to count backwards so that 435BC was longer ago that 25BC!

Look at this thermometer. Can you see how the temperatures below zero increase but have a minus sign before them?

100° 90° 80° 70° 60° 50° 40° 30° 20° 10° 0° -10° -20° -30°

## ACTIVITY

***Study the thermometer and answer these questions.***

1. Is 2°C warmer or colder than –3°C ?
2. Is –1°C warmer or colder than –4°C ?
3. One day in December the temperature outside was 4°C. Overnight the temperature fell by 5°C. What was the overnight temperature?

## ACTIVITY

Now draw your own thermometer in your notebook but instead of the temperatures, write in dates. Put 0 where the 0°C is and above it insert the years AD100, AD200, AD300, AD400 etc. Below the 0 insert the years 100BC, 200BC, 300BC, 400BC, etc. Now answer these questions.

1. Did 300BC come before or after AD100?
2. How many years are between 200BC and AD300?
3. Could someone born in AD10 have met someone who was born in 10BC?

This book is mostly about dates that are 'AD' so we won't bother putting AD in front of them. The Middle Ages are very, very interesting so let's go on a journey through them! Enjoy!

# UNIT 2: WHAT ARE THE MIDDLE AGES?

## THE DARK AGES

How do you know what is happening in the world? Write down as many ways as you can think of.

Now think of the ways in which we know about the people and events of many years ago. Are any of the methods the same? For example, could you read the web blog of the Roman Emperor Vespasian who lived around the year 70?

This book is about the Middle Ages (often called the **medieval** period). But what are they?

When someone is not very young and still not grey and wrinkled, they are called middle-aged. It's a bit like that with history. The term **Middle Ages** means simply the bit that comes between **Ancient History** (Julius Caesar, pyramids and things like that) and **Modern History** (Henry VIII, Hitler, First World War and things like that).

Historians have divided the Middle Ages into:

| | |
|---|---|
| **Early Middle Ages** | *about* **450 to 1000** |
| **High Middle Ages** | *about* **1000 to 1300** |
| **Late Middle Ages** | *about* **1300 to 1500** |

We have to talk about approximate dates because, throughout history, events don't always start and stop neatly. Something might go on from November 1262 until January 1264. Looking back to so long ago, we might just say it took place about 1263.

**APPROXIMATE: about, not exactly**

The Middle Ages, especially the Early Middle Ages, have sometimes been called **The Dark Ages**.

When a room is dark, it is hard or even impossible to see anything that is in it. Perhaps there isn't even a light that can be switched on in the room. The only way to see anything is if someone gets a torch and shines it around. Even then, you wouldn't see everything at once. You might see only a chair or a TV. You would see only the things that the torch lights up.

It's a bit like that with history. Some events in history, especially very recent history, are as clear as if they were floodlit. We can know almost everything about them. As we go further and further back in time, things get a little dimmer and we see only a few things clearly. Sometimes we can make out nothing at all.

**The only way to see anything is if someone gets a torch and shines it around.**

The American writer, naturalist and philosopher, Henry David Thoreau (1817–1862) said of the Middle Ages:

*"They are dark ... because we are so in the dark about them."*

From about the 14th century there was a great renewal of art, writing and culture in Europe. This was called the **Renaissance.** When historians looked back from this time, it seemed to them that there had been a very dark period when art, literature and learning struggled to survive at all.

There are three main reasons why the Middle Ages are sometimes called the Dark Ages.

## 1. THE ROMANS WITHDREW FROM BRITAIN

The Roman Empire covered a huge part of the known world for hundreds of years. They successfully invaded Britain in the year 55 and the Roman way of life spread across the country.

**KNOWN WORLD: the parts of the world then known to Europeans, ie Europe, western Asia and northern Africa.**

- They built forts and defensive walls to keep out invaders.
- Wealthy Romans built fine villas (large country houses) to live in.
- They built good straight roads for their armies to march quickly from one part of the country to another.
- They brought in their own governors and laws.
- Fine goods were traded from all over the Empire.

Then, in the early 5th century, Rome itself, and other parts of the Empire, came under attack and the armies in Britain were needed elsewhere. Rome decided to abandon Britain and withdrew its army.

All the government, law and civilisation that Rome had brought to Britain slowly fell apart:

- Native tribes, which had mostly been kept under control by the Romans, began to fight each other again.
- The good roads were not maintained and fell into disrepair.
- Other peoples, such as the Anglo-Saxons and the Vikings, were able to invade Britain.

The Romans had built in stone and we have plenty of archaeological evidence for their time in Britain. But there is very little surviving archaeology of the centuries immediately after Roman times.

The surviving parts of a Roman amphitheatre at Caerleon, near Newport in Wales. It would have been used mostly by soldiers who were stationed in the area.

What was an amphitheature used for?

A surviving Roman arch in Lincoln, England which was built in the 3rd century. It was once one of the main gates to the city. In 1964 it was badly damaged by a tall lorry, but fortunately the damage could be repaired.

*'Did the Roman armies invade Ireland? The answer is no, but we know they did consider it. During a foray into southern Scotland, the Roman General Agricola looked across the North Channel towards the Irish coast. The writer Tacitus reports that Agricola "saw that Ireland... conveniently situated for the ports of Gaul might prove a valuable acquisition" and that "I have often heard Agricola declare that a single legion, with a moderate band of auxiliaries, would be enough to finish the conquest of Ireland". However an invasion never took place – not because the Irish would be too hard to defeat, but simply because the Romans decided it wouldn't be worth the effort.'*

*Extract from: www.wesleyjohnston.com/users/ireland/past/pre_norman_history/iron_age.html, accessed 7 Jan 2011*

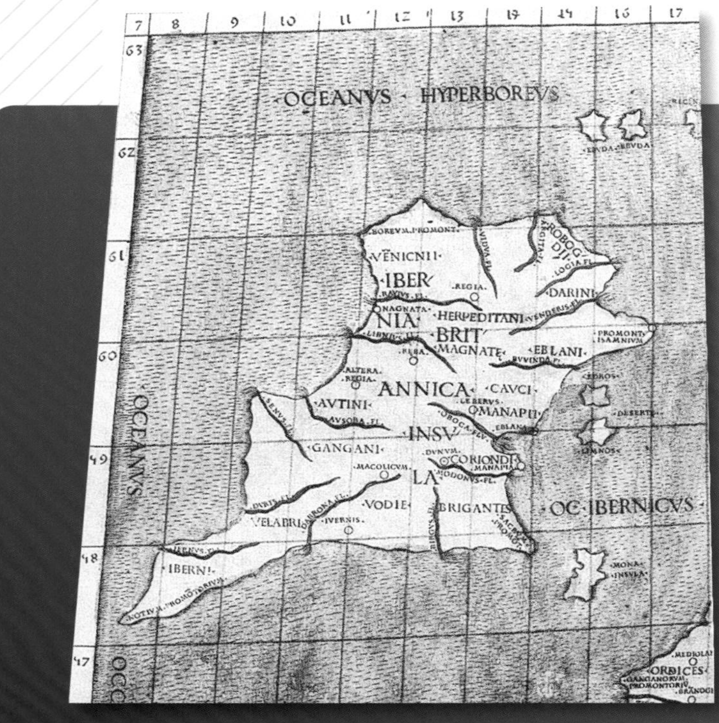


This is a copy of a map of Ireland, drawn from a description by the geographer Ptolemy. He lived in the 2nd century in Alexandria in Egypt, which was part of the Roman Empire. The original map was drawn about the year 120 but copies exist from the 15th century. Ptolemy never visited Ireland.

How might he have gathered his information?

TPD

Although the Romans never conquered Ireland, it was influenced by them. Merchants traded round the coasts and there were raiding parties to capture slaves to work on the Roman estates in Britain. When the Romans left Britain, their influence remained in Ireland in, for example, religion and the Latin language.

**CONQUERED: defeated in battle.**

## 2. THE CHRISTIAN RELIGION DECLINED

The Roman Empire provided trade routes along which the new religion of Christianity spread. Christianity arrived in Britain and the church organised and converted many of the native pagan people. Once the Romans left, Christianity began to decline and the pagan religions took hold again in many places.

This was important because Christian monasteries were places of learning. The monks copied out manuscripts, taught and passed on learning from one generation to the next. They came under attack from new invaders, especially the Vikings. Monasteries were burnt, the monks were massacred and many manuscripts were destroyed.

Here is an example of the beautiful work that was done by monks in monasteries in Early Middle Ages. This is from the Book of Kells and is the first page of the Gospel of John in the Bible. Pages decorated like this are called **illuminated** pages. The Book of Kells was created by Celtic monks about 800 and is kept in the Library of Trinity College Dublin.

## ACTIVITY

You could have a go at designing an illuminated page of your own.

## 3. LESS WRITTEN HISTORY SURVIVES

Compared to more modern history, there are fewer surviving sources that tell us what was happening during those hundreds of years after the Romans left.

However, there are some writers who shine torches for us into the darkness of this period of history and let us get glimpses of the life and times of these people who lived so long ago. We will look at some of them later, as we learn about the times they lived in.

*Just because it seemed like a dark time in Britain and Europe, it was not necessarily the same in other parts of the world. In the Arab world and in China, there were great advances in science, literature and astronomy.*

When you are studying a written source, you need to ask the following questions:

1. When was this written?
2. Who wrote it?
3. Why did they write it?
4. For whom was it written?
5. Are there reasons why the writer might hold a particular opinion on what they are describing?

## SOURCE

Read these two opinions.

***"Between the far away past history of the world, and that which lies near to us; in the time when the wisdom of the ancient times was dead and had passed away, and our own days of light had not yet come, there lay a great black gulf in human history, a gulf of ignorance, of superstition, of cruelty, and of wickedness. That time we call the dark or Middle Ages."***

Howard Pyle (1853–1911), American illustrator and writer

***"Those who suggest that the 'dark ages' were a time of violence and superstition would do well to remember the appalling cruelties of our own time, truly without parallel in past ages…"***

Jacques Le Goff (born 1924), French medieval historian

1. Do these two writers agree with each other? Explain your answer.
2. What do you think Howard Pyle meant by 'the wisdom of ancient times'?
3. Does Le Goff regard 'dark ages' as a good name for the Middle Ages? How can you tell?
4. When reading a source, is it important to know when the writer of the passage lived? Why or why not?

INTRODUCTION

# UNIT 3: BIAS

## WHAT IS BIAS?

When a speaker or writer tries to make his audience think in one particular way, it is called being **biased.**

## ACTIVITY

Read this account of a public meeting.

***"The speaker slouched up to the podium and dumped his notes down. I looked at the people around me in the audience. They were as starry-eyed as if their favourite tatty pop star had just said hello to them personally. The speaker shoved back his greasy hair and coughed. What an awful tie!"***

Another reporter wrote this about the same meeting:

***"It was obvious that the speaker was nervous as he made his way to the podium. Nevertheless, he set his notes firmly in front of him and looked steadily at his expectant audience. He smoothed his hair and cleared his throat."***

PODIUM: A tall narrow reading desk at which the speaker stands.

Discuss each of these accounts. For each one, decide what impression of the speaker the writer wants to give his readers. Pick out words and phrases to support your answer.

WO

## ACTIVITY

**Triplets**

Discuss the following newspaper headlines and say which statements are **biased** and which are neutral.

Scarcely 100 people turned up for the protest

Nearly 100 people arrived to protest

About 100 people attended the protest meeting

NEUTRAL: not on one side or the other.

Valiant United make Rovers sweat for their narrow victory

Rovers beat United 2 -1 in close game

United no match for fighting Rovers side

Exhausted fox torn to pieces by vicious hounds

Hunting party celebrates magnificent kill

The hounds killed a fox in today's village hunt

In pairs, make up some triplets of your own.

## PRIMARY AND SECONDARY SOURCES

A **primary** source is one where the person writing or talking is actually a witness to what they are writing or talking about. It is sometimes called a 'first-hand' account.

A **secondary** source is one where the written or spoken report is by someone who wasn't a witness to what they are reporting.

Unlike the Middle Ages, today we have radio and television reports on events too. So a film of a major fire, for example, is a *primary* source for what happened. A news item on the fire, written by someone in the studio, is a *secondary* source, because it is 'second-hand'.

## ACTIVITY

Here are two accounts of the **same event** but they are told by two different people.

"Hi Becky, it's Sarah. Guess what? I just saw a car accident. I'm just at the corner of my road. Drama! I don't think anyone's badly hurt but it seems like a big deal anyway. This blue Fiesta pulled out of our street just as I got to the corner and a big white van coming along the main road whacked right into it! Brakes squealed and there was a loud crunch noise. I'm so close a piece of orange glass flew past my foot. The guy driving the van has jumped out and is shouting at the man in the Fiesta. He's really mad! ... I'm going to move round a bit ...The poor old guy in the car looks a bit out of it. He's a cut on his head and his nose is bleeding all down his chin. The poor guy! He's just looking out his window at the guy shouting. Lots of other people have stopped to watch too. Now a woman's come over and has a tissue to wipe the guy's chin. The van driver's got out a notebook and he's writing in it. Anyway, I'd better get on home. See you tomorrow."

**From:** becky@myplace.co.uk
**Subject: This afternoon!**
**Date:** 14 December 2010 16:19:47 GMT
**To:** josie53@herplace.co.uk

Hey Josie

How about coming round later to do that maths homework together? Had a call from Sarah this avo. She saw a big car smash on her way home. One old guy was badly injured, blood everywhere. He probably had to go to hospital. A white van had sideswiped his car and Sarah was so close glass went all round her. She was lucky not to be injured herself. Van drivers! It was probably his fault. Van drivers think they own the road!

C ya

Becky ☺

### Class discussion

Read the two accounts of the traffic accident again.

Talk about the differences between the two. In what ways do they differ?

If you wanted to know what really happened, whose account would you believe: Sarah's or Becky's? Explain your answer.

Which is the primary source and which is the secondary source?

Look back at the picture of Ptolemy's map on page 10.
Do you think it is a primary or a secondary source?

## ACTIVITY

Pick **one** of the following and write 150 – 200 words about what you saw.

- A man is walking his dog and he passes a huge stray dog that stops and growls at his smaller dog as if it is going to attack it. What happens?
- A mother is walking up the street, holding her toddler by the hand. The child trips and falls. The child has a badly cut lip and is crying hard. You go up to the woman to see if you can help. What happens?
- Your sister has just got her driving test and has been out for her first drive alone. Your dad is watching her come back and sees a big scrape right down the side of the car. What happens?
- You are just going into a music shop and see a security man stop a young guy coming out. You hear security man ask the guy to return to the shop. You go in after them. What happens?

When you have finished, read your account to a partner.

*At home, and without talking about it again,* your partner should write down what you told them, as if they are telling someone *else* what you saw.

Compare what you wrote with what your partner wrote. Are the two accounts different? If so, how are they different and why do you think this is?

## ACTIVITY

### Class discussion

Discuss the advantages and disadvantages of both primary and secondary sources. Which is better?

Think hard about this and don't assume anything!

# PROJECT

Form into groups of four or five.

Each person in the group should pick a newspaper and buy this newspaper every day for one week.

When you have collected all your newspapers, compare how each newspaper has reported two stories during the week.

Have the stories been reported very differently?

Do you find evidence of bias?

Can you conclude anything about the views of the different reporters?

As a group, compile a short report for a conference on 'Bias in the newspaper media'.

Plan your report carefully and allocate a task or section of the report to each person in the group.

Your report should have:

- an introduction
- an account of how you went about your research
- your findings
- your conclusions
- a list of the newspapers you used (these are your *sources*)

**ALLOCATE: give or set aside for a particular purpose**

Perhaps your teacher will ask some groups to read out their reports in class.

**Extension activity**

Widen your research to include television and Internet treatment of your chosen stories and write your report for a conference on 'Bias in the media'.

## Review your work

Did your group find this task interesting?

Did you personally enjoy the task? Why or why not?

Was any part of it particularly difficult?

Was there anything you think your group could have done better? If so, how could it be done better?

# END OF SECTION QUIZ

## Class Quiz!

Divide into two teams and decide on a prize for the winning team. If you get a question right, your team gets a point, but if you get a question wrong, you lose a point! So think carefully before you answer.

1. What does AD stand for? You must give the Latin words.
2. What is a primary source?
3. "I hate dogs because I was bitten by an Alsatian once". Is the person who said this biased or neutral?
4. "There are loads of writers who tell us about the events of the Middle Ages." True or false?
5. Give two questions you should ask when you are studying a source.
6. Name two types of thing that the Romans built in Britain.
7. What does it mean to describe an old manuscript as 'illuminated'?
8. What are the approximate dates of the High Middle Ages?
9. What do the terms 'CE' and 'BCE' mean?
10. In what century was the year 942?
11. In what year did the Romans invade Ireland?
12. Where is the Book of Kells kept?

## Word Check

Check out these words to make sure you can spell them.

**approximate**
**Britain**
**allocate**
**bias**
**manuscript**
**podium**
**astronomy**
**necessary**
**ancient**
**parallel**
**Celtic**
**monastery**
**religion**
**Christianity**
**governor**
**illuminate**
**calendar**
**pyramid**
**Emperor**
**civilisation**
**Ireland**

If you're not sure if you can spell any of them, check them out a few more times.

# THE EARLY MIDDLE AGES
# UNIT 4: SOURCES OF INFORMATION

## THE ANGLO-SAXONS

The year **1066** was a big year in history – in this part of the world anyway. It was the year in which the Normans successfully invaded England and a whole way of life and government changed.

We will go on to investigate this period, but first it is important to know a little bit about England as it was in the years before the Normans came. The English people before 1066 were a blend of several groups who came as invaders – the **Celts** (up until about 100 BC), the **Anglo-Saxons** (from the mid 5th to the mid 7th centuries) and the **Vikings** (late 8th century to the 10th century). The Romans had also invaded, but did not settle in large numbers. England is named after the **Angles** (Anglo-Saxons) whose land was called **Angleland.** If you say it quickly it becomes England. The French name for England is still **Angleterre.**

The Anglo-Saxon period stretched from the collapse of Roman rule in Britain up to the Norman invasion in 1066. We don't have as much first-hand information on the Anglo-Saxons as we do for later times. Historians can use several things as evidence to work out what life was like. For example, old burial sites give clues if there are items buried with the person.

## ACTIVITY

What conclusions could an archaeologist draw from the following burials?

1. A child's grave with a wooden spinning top and the bones of a dog.
2. A man's grave with knives, a spear and a musical pipe made from animal horn.
3. A woman's grave with needles, weaving tools and some bone beads.
4. A large burial with a man's skeleton, gold brooches, decorated gold sword hilts, silver decorations from a horse's harness and a very finely made battle helmet.

## THE ANGLO-SAXON CHRONICLE

The **Anglo-Saxon Chronicle** is a very important source for the history of the Middle Ages. It is thought that it was begun about 890, on the orders of King Alfred the Great and some copies were still being updated into the early 12th century. None of the original manuscripts survive, but many copies were made and distributed to the libraries of different monasteries. These copies were updated separately, so not all the copies that do survive are exactly the same.

When it was first started, it was written in Anglo-Saxon English, also known as Old English. This is interesting to historians of language because, as you read through the Chronicle, the development of the English language can be traced.

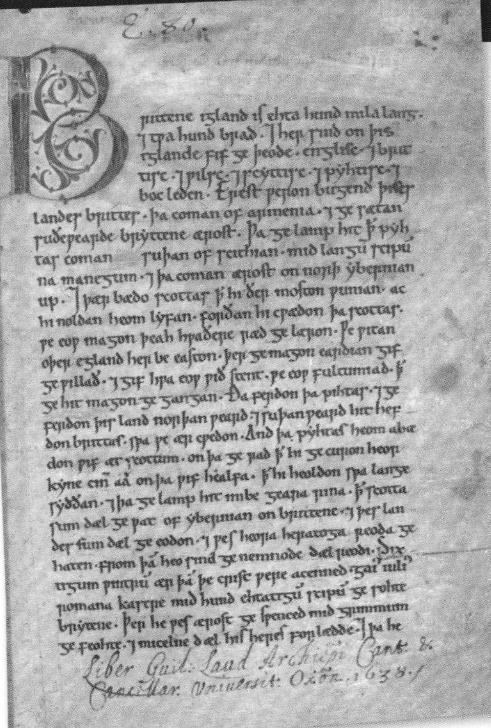

This is the first page of a copy of the Anglo-Saxon Chronicle. This copy is called the Peterborough Chronicle.

The Anglo-Saxon Chronicle is also important because of its **viewpoint.**

The people who wrote the Anglo-Saxon Chronicle were ordinary Anglo-Saxon scribes, usually monks, who recorded the history of their country regardless of whose side they were on. We'll look at some of the things they wrote as we learn more about the Middle Ages. Here is a typical example of an entry:

**SCRIBE: a writer who copied manuscripts or took dictation from others.**

*AD946. This year King Edmund died, on St. Augustine's mass day. That was widely known, how he ended his days: – that Leof stabbed him at Pucklechurch. And Ethelfleda of Damerham, daughter of Alderman Elgar, was then his queen. And he reigned six years and a half: and then succeeded to the kingdom Edred Atheling his brother, who soon after reduced all the land of the Northumbrians to his dominion; and the Scots gave him oaths, that they would do all that he desired.*

## ACTIVITY

Using a word processing program, write out the event described as a headline story for a modern local newspaper. Use your imagination! Include interviews with those involved and with witnesses. Add in photographs if you can, or indicate what your photographs would be. Remember to make up a good headline that will grab attention.

*History isn't just about events. Language has history too and develops and changes over the centuries.*

*For example, 'awful' used to mean 'wonderful, filled with awe'.*

*'brave' used to mean 'cowardly'*
*'nice' used to mean 'ignorant' or 'stupid'*
*'a wireless' was a radio*
*'silly' used to mean 'blessed' or 'happy'*

# UNIT 5: THE VENERABLE BEDE

**VENERABLE:** worth respecting because of great age or excellent character.

**The Venerable Bede**

Bede was born in 673 in Northumberland in the north of England. Apart from one or two visits to friends, he spent all of his life as a monk in a monastery at Jarrow. He is very important to historians today because of a book he wrote, called *The Ecclesiastical History of the English People*. This is an account of Christianity in England almost up to Bede's own time. However, it is also a main source for the history of these years in England. In fact, Bede's writings are so important that he has been called 'the Father of English History'.

Bede was first and foremost a churchman, and he wrote many commentaries on books of the Bible. His theological writings were popular all over Europe and monasteries kept copies of them in their libraries. One Bishop said of Bede that he "shone forth as a lantern in the church by his scriptural commentary".

He also wrote poetry and about music and science. He was one of the most educated men in Europe at the time and said of himself: "It has always been my delight to learn or to teach or to write".

Bede was the first person to refer to dates as being 'AD'. In his writing he used the phrase 'anno domini', meaning 'the year of our Lord'. As you read in Unit 1, we still use this today.

On the day Bede died, 26 May 735, he was still working. He finished his translation of the Gospel of John into English by dictating it to a scribe. He was buried in Jarrow but in the 11th century his body was moved to the Norman Cathedral in Durham.

## ACTIVITY

Read the following passage. It is Bede's description of Ireland. Answer the questions that follow.

*"Ireland is the greatest island next to Britain, and lies to the west of it; but as it is shorter than Britain to the north, so, on the other hand, it runs out far beyond it to the south, opposite to the northern parts of Spain, though a spacious sea lies between them…*

*Ireland, in breadth, and for wholesomeness and serenity of climate, far surpasses Britain; for the snow scarcely ever lies there above three days: no man makes hay in the summer for winter's provision, or builds stables for his beasts of burden. No reptiles are found there, and no snake can live there; for, though often carried thither out of Britain, as soon as the ship comes near the shore, and the scent of the air reaches them, they die. On the contrary, almost all things in the island are good against poison. In short, we have known that when some persons have been bitten by serpents, the scrapings of leaves of books that were brought out of Ireland, being put into water, and given them to drink, have immediately expelled the spreading poison, and assuaged the swelling. The island abounds in milk and honey, nor is there any want of vines, fish, or fowl; and it is remarkable for deer and goats."*

Bede, *Ecclesiastical History of the English People*

**ASSUAGED: helped to make better.**

1. If the writer had not mentioned Ireland, would you have guessed he was describing it?
2. Is Bede correct in his geographical location of Ireland? Explain your answer.
3. What sort of climate does Bede describe? What could you conclude from this?
4. How could Bede have obtained his information?
5. Imagine this passage is an article in a newspaper. Write a headline for it.

## ACTIVITY

TPD

You have to write a physical description of Ireland for an historian living 1500 years in the future. Don't write about events; just describe the island and its people. Write 150–200 words.

Think about what is important for an historian to know. What could you include in your description that Bede would not have been able to include?

Compare your description to others in the class. Have others given very different descriptions to yours?

If so, what are the differences and are there any reasons for them?

## ACTIVITY

Look at this painting.

**DEATHBED: where somebody rests in the final hours before they die.**

This is a painting of Bede on his deathbed. It was painted by JD Penrose in 1902.

1. Describe what you see.
2. What do you think is happening in the picture?
3. Apart from Bede, who do you think the others in the picture are?
4. There are several items in the room. See how many of them you can identify and say what they were for.
5. How likely is this to be an accurate picture of Bede on the day he died? Explain your answer.
6. As a result of your discussion, do you think this picture is a primary or a secondary source?

# UNIT 6: RULERS AND RELIGION

## THE SEVEN KINGDOMS

Before the Vikings came in 793, Anglo-Saxon England was divided into smaller kingdoms. The seven main ones were Northumbria, Mercia, Wessex, Kent, East Anglia, Essex, and Sussex. These seven kingdoms have come to be called **The Heptarchy.** The prefix 'hept-' means seven.

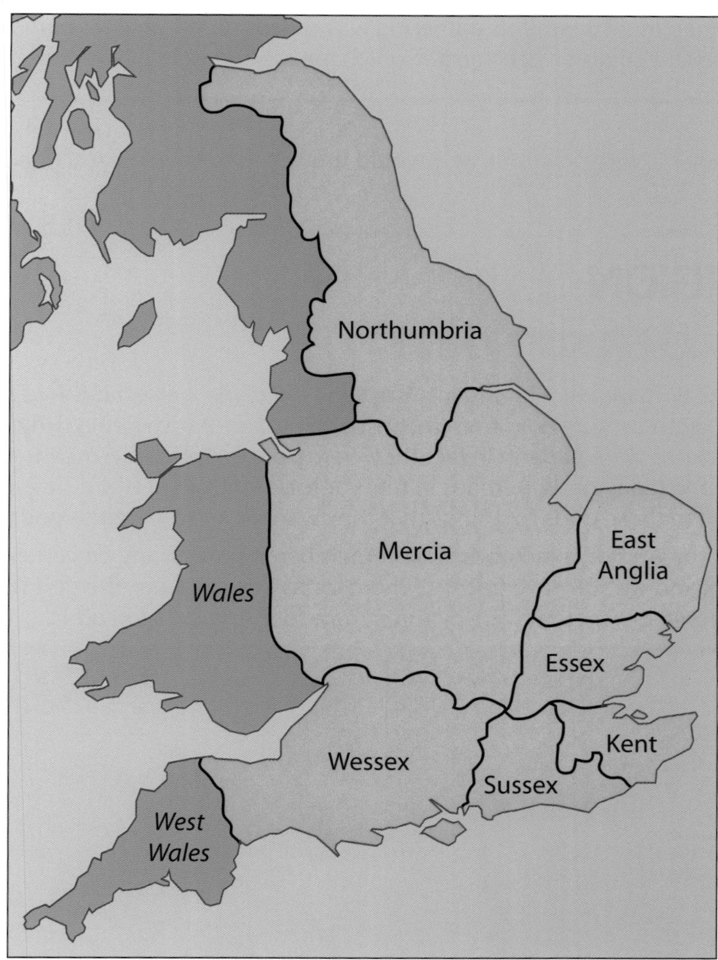


This map shows how England was divided into smaller Anglo-Saxon kingdoms.

Each of these kingdoms was ruled by a king, but it wasn't a hereditary monarchy like England is today. The strongest chief of the area held his lands by the power of his army. He gave plunder, land and slaves to his supporters and they, in turn, continued to fight for him. To be a strong leader, you had to be able to fight in battles and hold onto your lands by force. When a king died, anyone could try to succeed him. The kingdoms that became most powerful were Northumbria, Mercia and Wessex.

**PLUNDER: items of value that have been taken from a defeated enemy.**

## ACTIVITY

### Class discussion

Do you think that the Anglo-Saxon way of deciding who would be king was a good one? To help you decide, draw a line down the middle of a page and in one column write 'Strengths' and in the other write 'Weaknesses'. When you have finished your lists, discuss your conclusions.

To advise him, a king gathered round him the most powerful nobles and churchmen in the land. This gathering was called the **Witan.** This name comes from the Old English *witena gemōt* which means "meeting of wise men".

If someone is very powerful, why would they need to have advisors?

# RELIGION

## ANGLO-SAXON GODS

When the Romans were in Britain, Christianity became well established as a religion. St Patrick (5th century) was from a Christian Romano-British family. However, the Anglo-Saxons were pagans. In fact they were **polytheistic.** This means that they worshipped many gods, perhaps in trees or rocks or even at wells. They prayed and sacrificed to these gods for things that they wanted, or to keep the gods happy.

**ROMANO-BRITISH: native people in Britain who had a Roman lifestyle.**

Some of the Anglo-Saxon gods were remembered particularly on certain days of the week and we still have traces of them today. For example, the god Tiw was remembered on 'Tiwsday'. The pictures show four Anglo-Saxon gods.

Tiw

Odin

Thor

Freyja

## ACTIVITY

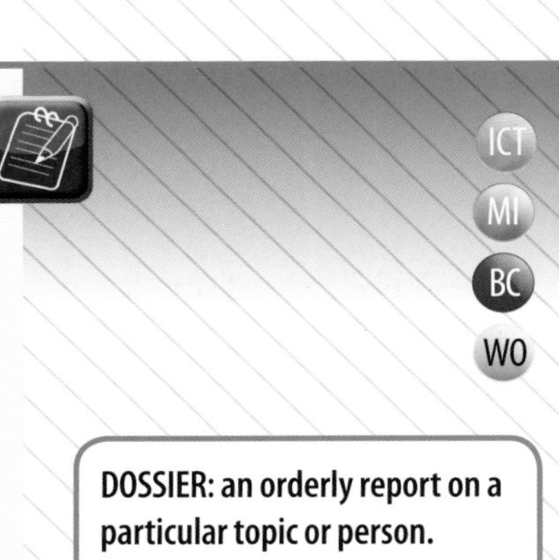


Odin, Thor, and Freyja are three other gods whose names are preserved in days of the week.

In pairs, pick one of these gods and find out all you can about them.

Plan and put together a dossier of information on your chosen god. You should include:

- a cover page
- a drawing or painting
- an introduction
- main description
- a conclusion
- an index
- a list of the places where you got your information (these are your sources)

When you have finished, swap your dossier with another pair who studied a different god. Write some brief comments about their report, saying what you found interesting and **one** thing that you felt could have been done better.

## CHRISTIANITY

In 597 Augustine, a missionary from Rome, landed in Kent. Aethelbert was the king of Kent at that time. The passage below is Bede's account of what happened. Remember that Bede was writing this about 730. (Don't worry about the three dots like this – ... it just means that a few words have been left out.)

*"In this island landed the servant of our Lord, Augustine, and his companions, being as is reported, nearly forty men ...Sending to Aethelbert they signified that they were come from Rome, and brought a joyful message...*

*The king, having heard this, ordered them to stay in that island where they had landed and that they should be furnished with all necessaries till he should consider what to do with them. For he had heard of the Christian religion, having a Christian wife, of the royal family of the Franks, called Bertha...*

*The king came into the island and, sitting in the open air, ordered Augustine and his companions to be brought into his presence. For he had taken precaution that they should not come to him in any house, lest, according to an ancient superstition, they practice any magical arts they might impose upon him, and so get the better of him. ...*

*When Augustine had sat down... and preached to him and his attendants there present the word of life, the king answered thus: "Your words and promises are very fair, but they are new to us and of uncertain import, and I cannot approve of them so far as to forsake that which I have so long followed with the whole English nation. But because you are come from far into my kingdom, and, as I conceive, are desirous to impart to us those things which you believe to be true and most beneficial, we will not molest you, but give you favourable entertainment and take care to supply you with the necessary sustenance; nor do we forbid you to preach and gain as many as you can to your religion."*

A painting of Augustine preaching to Aethelbert. It was painted in 1864.

# ACTIVITY

**Comprehension**

Read over the extract from Bede, and study the picture of the scene that Bede described.

Now answer these questions.

1. What does the picture tell you that the written account does not?
2. What does the written account tell you that the picture does not?
3. Which tells you more about this event – the picture or the written account?
4. How do you imagine Augustine felt about meeting Aethelbert?
5. How did King Aethelbert treat Augustine and his companions? How can you tell?
6. Why did Aethelbert want to meet Augustine in the open air?
7. Bede gives one reason why Aethelbert may have decided to listen to Augustine. What is it?
8. The king was furious and ordered Augustine to stop talking about Christianity. True or false?
9. What does "they should be furnished with all necessaries" mean?
10. Are you surprised by Aethelbert's response to Augustine? Why or why not?
11. Are there any clues to Bede's own viewpoint in his account of the incident? If so, what are they?
12. Bede describes Augustine as having 'companions' and the king as having 'attendants'. Do you think the choice of these different words is significant? If so, why?
13. Which of these three statements is correct?
    (a) These are both primary sources.
    (b) These are both secondary sources.
    (c) Bede's account is a primary source and the picture is a secondary source.

**ARCHBISHOP: the most senior bishop of the land.**

**CATHEDRAL: the church where a bishop or archbishop was based.**

Canterbury Cathedral as it looks today.

Aethelbert gave Augustine land in Canterbury to build a church. Canterbury became the main centre for English Christianity. Augustine would have built something small, probably made from wood. You can see in the photograph how much this changed over the centuries!

Today it is the most important centre for the Anglican Church. Augustine became the first Archbishop of Canterbury. In 1993, archaeologists uncovered the remains of the original Anglo-Saxon building and discovered that it had been built right across an old Roman road.

You can find out much more about Canterbury Cathedral at the web site: canterbury-cathedral.org

Who is the present Archbishop of Canterbury?

Most of the churches built at this time were of wood so nothing remains of them, except perhaps some traces of their foundations. There is one very well preserved stone Anglo-Saxon church in England, at Escomb in Co Durham. It has been in use almost continuously since Anglo-Saxon times. It was founded about 670.

Escombe church as it looks today.

# UNIT 7: EVERYDAY LIFE

## HOUSES

Compared to today, the population of Anglo-Saxon England was small. Most ordinary people lived in small villages and worked on farms. A village might have less than a hundred people in it.

Here is a picture of a peasant's house with some of the walls taken away so that we can see inside. On the right is a low wall separating the people from the animals, who also lived in the house for safety and warmth.

## ACTIVITY

1. Discuss this picture. What do you see?
2. Describe how you think this house was built and what materials were used. What problems would there be in building and maintaining a house like this?
3. If you had to live in this house, make a list of things that you would miss most from your life today. Rank order your list, putting a '1' beside the thing you would miss most, '2' beside the next and so on. Compare your own preferences with others in the class. How are they different?
4. There is a boy in the picture, feeding a cow. What do you think *he* would feel about *your* house? For example, would he like to sleep in a room on his own instead of sleeping in one room with all his family? Would he recognise anything in your house?

## ACTIVITY

Write a story based on this picture. Write 300 – 500 words. To plan your story, ask questions such as: Who are these people? What time of day is it? What is happening? What might be about to happen?

Perhaps your teacher could pick some of your stories to read out.

# FOOD

**FORGE: a place where metal work was carried out, such as making horseshoes or armour.**

Anglo-Saxon kings and powerful nobles lived in settlements like small estates, where there was a hall with smaller buildings around it for the noblemen and slaves and for the kitchens, forge and so on. This hall was built of wood also, but was big enough to hold feasts and council gatherings. There was a fire in the middle and a hole in the roof to let the smoke out. It might be decorated on the walls with the heads of animals that had been hunted and perhaps with colourful tapestries. If a king or a rich nobleman wanted to keep the loyalty of his people, he was expected to give lavish feasts and entertainments.

Many fruit and vegetables that we take for granted now were unknown in Anglo-Saxon times. For example, potatoes weren't known in Britain until the 1580s. The Anglo-Saxons didn't know about oranges or bananas or kiwi fruit.

*Potato plants were brought back from Virginia, in North America, by the first colonists. The first potatoes in the British Isles were planted in Youghal in Co Cork, Ireland, by Sir Walter Raleigh, about 1586. They were eaten in Ireland for a while before the English realised how tasty they were!*

People couldn't just go down to McDonalds for a burger or to the shops for something for lunch. They had to grow or hunt everything they ate. They grew wheat, oats, rye and barley. They also grew lentils, peas and beans. There was very little free time.

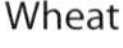

Wheat

Rye

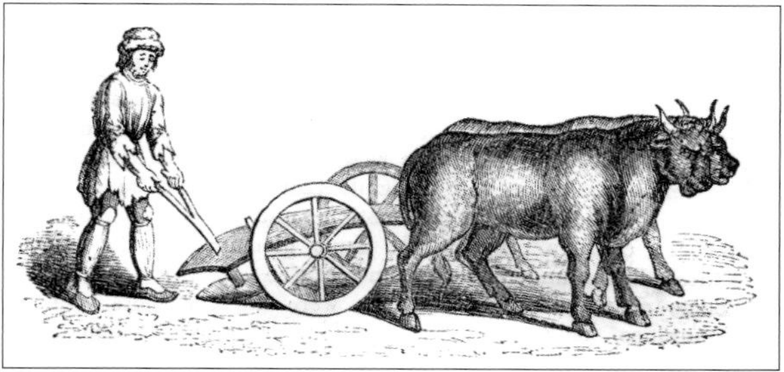

They kept animals for food, labour and for the materials to make their clothing. Here are the most common ones, and what they were used for:

- oxen: large strong cattle for pulling the plough
- sheep: lamb, mutton, sheep's milk, wool
- goats: milk, meat
- pigs: meat
- chickens: eggs and meat
- geese: eggs and meat
- bees: honey

Milk was used to make cheese and butter. There was no sugar so honey was important as a sweetener.

## ACTIVITY
### Class discussion

Think about the consequences of living like this.
If you grew up in an Anglo-Saxon village, could you do all the things that you do today? Could you have ambitions for your future career?
What would an Anglo-Saxon boy or girl think of the way you live?

## SLAVERY

The Anglo-Saxon way of life included slaves. They were at the bottom of the social hierarchy. You could become a slave if you were defeated in battle or perhaps if you owed money for something and couldn't pay, you would have to become a slave as a way of paying what you owed. It was possible to be freed once you had worked off the debt. Of course, you might be born into slavery because your mother was a slave.

Sometimes if times were very bad, such as during a famine, a family might have to sell one of their children into slavery.

**HIERARCHY: where people or things are ranked one above the other according to status.**

This would bring money into the family, but can you think of another reason why a family might sell a child?

## CLOTHES

Peasants made their clothes from wool or animal skins. Women had to spend a lot of time spinning the wool from sheep and goats to make thread and then weaving the thread into cloth on a loom. Men wore tunics, with trousers or leggings that were tied round the legs with strips of cloth or leather. This was called cross-gartering.

Anglo-Saxon women wore long dresses, usually with a belt at the waist and perhaps fastened at the shoulder with a brooch.

Richer people could use silk as well. This was expensive because it had to be imported from Far Eastern countries and would be brought round the country by traders. Wealthy nobles could also have much finer jewellery. Anglo-Saxon jewellery was very fine indeed and they had very skilled craftsmen.

Here is an example of a silver brooch which dates from the late 9th century. It is called the *Fuller Brooch*.

### ACTIVITY

Find pictures of some more Anglo-Saxon brooches.

Do you see any similarity in style? What characteristics do they have?

Now you can design and draw or paint your own Anglo-Saxon brooch!

You could put your designs up as a display in the classroom.

### ACTIVITY

Use the Internet to find out about the Anglo-Saxon village reconstructed at West Stow in Suffolk, England.

When you have finished, share in class your thoughts about what it would be like to live there.

Is there anything else you would like to know about Anglo-Saxon village life? If so, try to find out about it and share your findings with the class.

# UNIT 8: SUTTON HOO

## SUTTON HOO

One of the barrows at Sutton Hoo.

One of the most amazing finds ever made relating to the Anglo-Saxons was discovered at Sutton Hoo, near Woodbridge in Suffolk, England. There are eleven mounds, called barrows, close together. In 1939, the largest of these was excavated – and what a find it turned out to be! It was a complete ship burial, full of artifacts that dated from the early 7th century.

**EXCAVATE: dig carefully in order to find out what's beneath**

## ACTIVITY

Use a map to find the location of Sutton Hoo.

Draw a coloured sketch map of Suffolk, showing the main towns, rivers and Sutton Hoo.

All the wood of the ship had rotted away but it was possible to see the outline of the ship preserved in the soil. Nearly all of the iron rivets which held the planking together were still in place.

This burial held a huge amount of gold and silver artifacts from the early Anglo-Saxon age. There were gold buckles from belts, silver drinking vessels and spoons, shoulder clasps with intricate designs, a sword still in its scabbard (a long, thin protective covering for a sword), and even a lyre (a musical instrument).

Archaeologists working at Sutton Hoo in 1939.

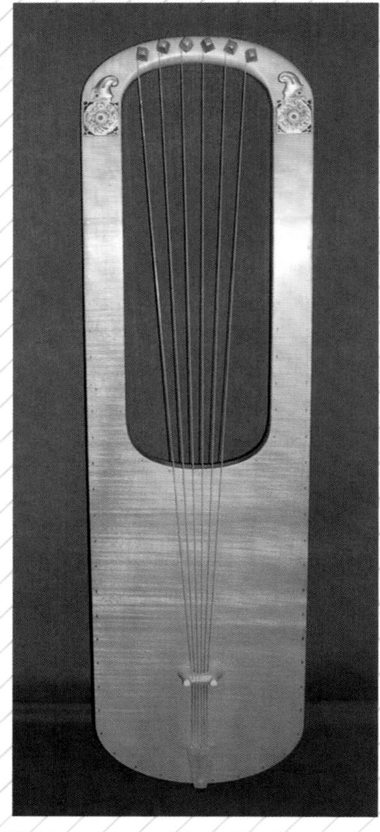

This is a reconstruction of the lyre which was found in the burial.

This is a finely decorated belt buckle.

On the left is the remains of a beautiful ceremonial helmet that was found beside where the head of the body would have been. The helmet was wrapped in cloth. (The body itself did not survive.)
On the right is a reconstruction of the helmet.

BC

## ACTIVITY

Draw a copy of this helmet and label each of the parts, saying what the purpose of each part was.

# UNIT 9: THE VIKINGS

## THE ARRIVAL OF THE VIKINGS

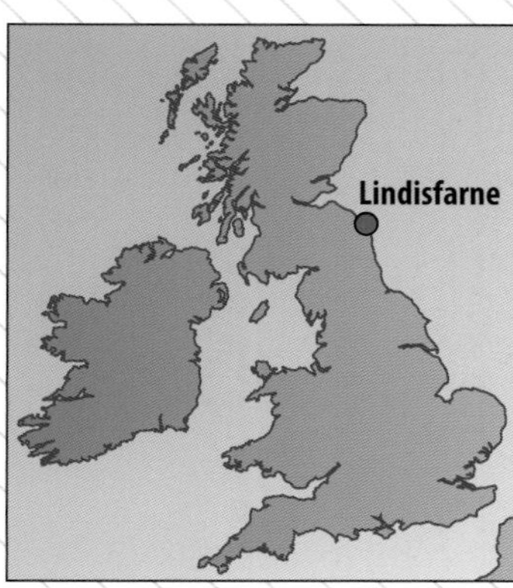


It is important to realise that in the Early Middle Ages, Britain and Ireland were influenced by the Scandinavian countries (much more than they are today). This was largely because of the Vikings who came from there to invade and plunder round the coasts of Britain and Ireland.

The first attack by the Vikings was in 793, at the monastery of Lindisfarne, also called Holy Island, off the east coast of England. Most historians regard this event as the beginning of the Viking age. This is the entry in the Anglo-Saxon Chronicle:

> *AD793. This year came dreadful fore-warnings over the land of the Northumbrians, terrifying the people most woefully: these were immense sheets of light rushing through the air, and whirlwinds, and fiery dragons flying across the firmament. These tremendous tokens were soon followed by a great famine: and not long after, on the sixth day before the ides of January in the same year, the harrowing inroads of heathen men made lamentable havoc in the church of God in Holy-island, by rapine and slaughter.*

**IDES: an old word meaning the middle day of a month.**

This is what Alcuin, a scholar in Northumbria at the time, wrote:

> *Never before has such terror appeared in Britain as we have now suffered from a pagan race... The heathens poured out the blood of saints around the altar, and trampled on the bodies of saints in the temple of God, like dung in the streets.*

**SIMILIE: a figure of speech where two things are compared using 'like' or 'as'.**

Can you see a simile in the quotation from Alcuin? Do you think it is a good simile for Alcuin to use here? Why or why not?

## ACTIVITY

BC

Imagine that you are a young boy or girl who was walking along the shore near Lindisfarne. You look out sea and discover that there are three Viking longboats full of armed warriors heading towards the land. You must warn the monks and try to escape.

Write a diary entry describing what happened and what you did.

## ACTIVITY

Form into groups of about four.

Each group should imagine that it is one of the monks at Lindisfarne.

Note that:

- there are about sixty monks in the monastery.
- some of the monks are very old and not able to move fast.
- some of the monks are novices with little experience.
- the monastery contains some children who have been sent there to be educated.
- the monastery contains many irreplaceable treasures of gold and other precious stones.
- there is no fortified wall around the monastery.
- the monastery has a library of fine manuscripts; all have been hand copied and some are intricately decorated.

You have been warned about the Vikings who will land in about an hour and who will start to attack the monastery.

Write out a list of dangers that you foresee.

Write out a list of actions that you could take. Remember – you have an hour!

Now put your actions in the order in which you would carry them out and say which danger this will address.

Compare the decisions of your group with the other groups. Are there any differences?

The Viking threat unified the Anglo-Saxons. The first Anglo-Saxon king to conquer and rule all of England was **Alfred the Great** (849–899). He is one of the most famous kings of all. You will research King Alfred in Unit 13.

His successors ruled England until Vikings from Denmark (the Danes) conquered the country in 1014. The Danes made **Canute** King of England as well as of Denmark. Canute reigned from 1016 until 1035.

# KING CANUTE

To secure his hold on the English throne, Canute married Emma, the widow of the previous Anglo-Saxon king. Later he also became King of Norway, so when he died at the age of about 40 in 1035 he ruled three kingdoms – Denmark, Norway and England. When Canute died, his sons fell out among themselves and his empire was divided. The English took the opportunity to restore an Anglo-Saxon king.

Although he fought battles and took over land, Canute was a Christian and did not approve of the things that his Viking forefathers had done. In order to show respect to his English subjects, he apologised for some of the things that had happened in the past. He built churches and gave gifts to monasteries and churches as well. Because he ruled the Viking countries, he was able to stop them raiding England and there were nearly twenty years of peace.

*Peace is important for a civilisation to flourish. Think about what happens to matters such as trade routes, art, ideas, families, travel, education and so on, during times of war.*

There is a famous story about Canute.

Courtiers, whose positions at court depended on remaining important to the king and staying friends with him, surrounded him. So they would flatter him all the time, telling him how great he was, how strong a fighter, how everyone thought he was the best king who ever lived and that everyone and everything obeyed him.

Canute knew this wasn't true and he got fed up with hearing so much flattery. He asked his courtiers to carry his throne down to the beach. He sat down in it and commanded that the tide should not come in. He ordered the sea not to touch his feet.

Of course the tide did come in. Canute not only got his feet wet but his cloak and chair as well.

He turned to his rather alarmed courtiers and said: "Let all men know how empty and worthless is the power of kings. For there is none worthy of the name but God, whom heaven, earth and sea obey."

King Canute

## ACTIVITY

Explain in your own words what Canute was trying to teach his courtiers.

## ACTIVITY

BC

**Divide the class into about three groups.**

- Each group should write a script for a short play based on the story of Canute and the sea.
- Try to give a part to everyone in your group. Remember you can make up as many characters as you want. Research some Viking names for your characters.
- Perhaps you could include sound effects and props.
- If there is time, you could perform these plays in class.

# UNIT 10: IRELAND IN THE EARLY MIDDLE AGES

## IRISH SOCIETY

Unlike England, the Anglo-Saxons had not settled in Ireland. Its population was a mixture of Celts and Vikings. Most Irish people spoke the Gaelic language and followed Gaelic laws. The Vikings had raided the coasts of Ireland as well as England and formed settlements at Dublin, Waterford, Wexford, Cork and Limerick. Historians used to think that these became quite large Viking towns, but more recently archaeologists think that Dublin was the only large Viking settlement and the others were merely trading posts. Trade was mainly controlled by these five Viking settlements.

What factors might lead historians and archaeologists today to think that some of the Viking settlements were not as large as they used to think they were?

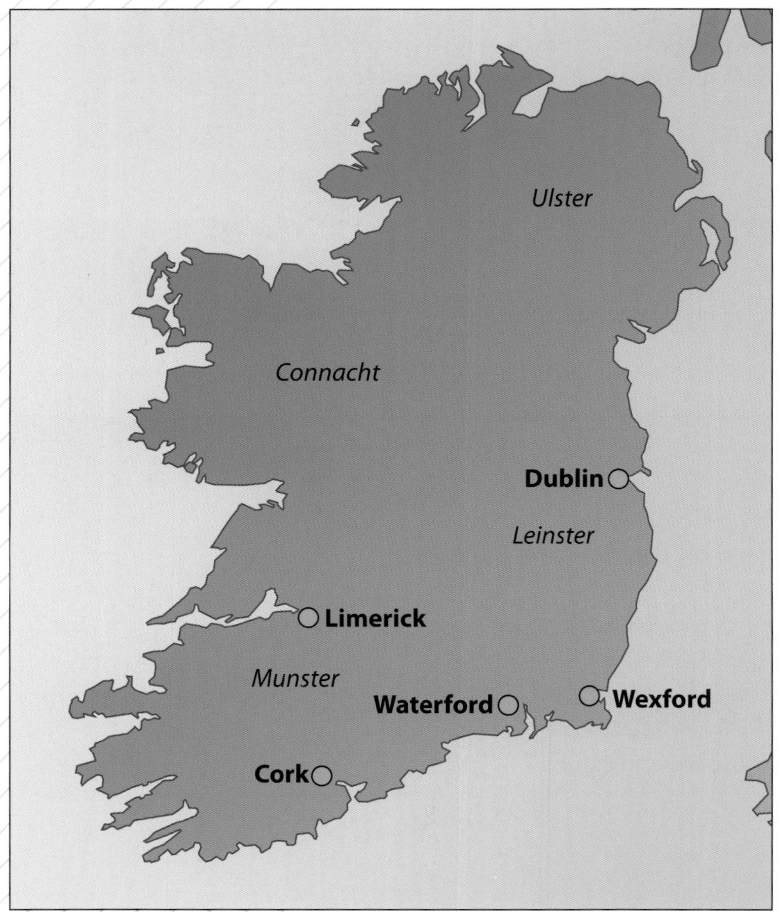


Celtic society was very complicated. Ireland was divided into several main territories each ruled by its own King. Each of these was divided further into sub-kingdoms each with its own ruler, who was subject to the main king.

The most powerful of these kings was called the **High King.** The High King was rather like a champion boxer. He remained High King only as long as he was unbeaten.

Viking settlements in Ireland and some of the main Irish kingdoms.

Unlike England, which had settled farming villages with people growing crops, Irish people made their living mostly by raising cattle. This meant that in some areas, particularly Ulster, the people were semi-nomadic.

**NOMADIC: moving around; not settling in one place for long.**

Most warfare consisted of cattle raiding, often over long distances, into another kingdom. Irishmen fought without armour, using short spears, javelins or large axes.

The Irish had no towns, apart from the Viking trading ports. Because they did not live in towns or farms, the Irish were often despised by English writers.

Gerald of Wales was a later writer who lived in the 12th century. You will learn more about him in Unit 19. Here is his description of Ireland:

> *They live on beasts... while man usually progresses from the woods to the fields to towns... this people despises agriculture... Cultivated fields are indeed few in number through the neglect of the cultivators: nevertheless the land is naturally fertile and fruitful.*

## ACTIVITY

The Irish did a lot of raiding of each other's cattle. There is a very early Irish story called *Táin Bó Cúailnge,* known in English as 'The Cattle Raid of Cooley'. It tells the story of a raid by Queen Medb (pronounced 'Mave') of Connacht into Ulster to capture a fine stud bull. Ulster is defended by the legendary hero Cú Chulainn (pronounced 'coo cullin').

This is a painting, created in 1911, showing Cú Chulainn of Ulster going into battle against Queen Medb of Connacht.

Describe it. Mention all the things that you see. Don't just describe things, describe the mood and the emotions that you see as well.

Do you think that an historian could come to any firm conclusions about the nature of Irish warfare just by studying this picture?

Why or why not?

## RELIGION

SCHOLAR: someone who is educated or enjoys studying.

Christianity had almost completely replaced the pagan religions in Ireland by around 600. Ireland was famous for its Celtic monasteries. They became major centres for maintaining the Christian religion and learning. In fact, missionaries were sent from Ireland to Britain and to other countries in Europe. Ireland became so famous for its learning that scholars and monks came to Ireland to study.

A reconstruction of a Celtic monastery at the Ulster History Park near Omagh, Co Tyrone. Unfortunately, this park is no longer open.

A High Cross: The Cross of the Scriptures, Clonmacnoise Monastery, Co Offaly

Their monastic buildings were very simple, just several small stone beehive-shaped cells for the monks to live in, clustered around a small stone church. When the Vikings began to attack, monasteries added a wall for protection around the whole settlement. High towers were built, although there is still some debate amongst historians about their purpose. Because they were built only after the Vikings started raiding Ireland, they may have been for storing holy treasures and for the monks to hide in. The Irish name for these towers is *cloigtheach* which means 'a bell house' so perhaps they were bell towers. It's also possible that they served both functions. Most monasteries had a **High Cross** like the one in the picture. High Crosses were very skillfully carved and are fine examples of the art of this time.

## ACTIVITY

**Drawing up a plan of action**

In pairs, imagine you are in charge of a monastery in 800. You want to build a tower as a protection against raiders.

Draw up a plan of action using these headings:

- The dangers we face
- Why we think a tower will be the best defence to build
- What features the tower needs to have to defend against the dangers
- Where we should build the tower
- What materials we will need
- What skills we will need to complete the task
- How we will find the money we need to build the tower

Once you have finished, swap your plan of action with another pair. Do you think they have thought of everything? Have they thought of anything you didn't think of? Did you think of anything they didn't think of?

What are the advantages of drawing up a plan of action before starting on a project?

## ACTIVITY

Here are some words from a 9th century Christian hymn:

*...Be thou my soul's shelter, be thou my strong tower...*
*O raise thou me heavenward, great Power of my power*
*High King of Heaven, thou heaven's bright sun...*
*O grant me its joys after victory is won.*

How can you tell that an Irish person wrote this hymn?

## PLACE NAMES

Because Ireland had so few settlements, place names developed by using the characteristics of the landscape. Here are some words that you might recognise as being part of some place names that you know. These words all come from the Irish language.

| PART OF PLACE NAME | MEANING |
|---|---|
| bally | homestead |
| beg | small |
| bun | river mouth |
| carrig/carrick | rocky outcrop |
| clough/clogh | rock |
| derry | oak grove |
| donagh/dona | church |
| drum/drom | ridge |
| glas/glass | green |
| inish/inch | island |
| knock | hill |
| letter | hillside |
| mona/money | peatland |
| more | big |
| mulla/mullagh | summit |
| rath/ra | ringfort |
| tra | beach |

### ACTIVITY

What do the following place names mean?

**Mullaghglass** **Carrickfergus** **Moneymore** **Inish Beg** **Ballymoney**

Note: Fergus was the name of a legendary king.

## ACTIVITY

Divide the class into teams.

Give each team a map of Ireland and see which team can identify the meaning of the most place names using the words given in the list. You must try to say what the names might mean.

This process happened in England too, and many English names come from the Old English language. Here are some examples:

| | |
|---|---|
| *burgh* | fortified town, borough |
| *burn* | stream |
| *bury* | fortified place |
| *stow* | meeting or holy place |
| *ham* | village |
| *ing* | people |
| *worth* | fenced land |

## ACTIVITY

Divide the class into teams.

Can you think of any names near where you live that might have come from more recent features? For example, in Omagh, Co Tyrone, there is a bridge called 'King James's Bridge'. In 1689, during the Williamite wars in Ireland, King James and his army crossed this bridge on their way to Derry. The name has stuck ever since.

# THE EARLY MIDDLE AGES CASE STUDY
# UNIT 11: BRIAN BORU

## BRIAN BORU

One person in Irish history whose name you must learn is Brian Boru. He was a very famous king and, unlike legendary heroes like Cú Chulainn, we know that Brian Boru was a real person.

He was born in what is now Co Clare about 941 and became King of Munster about 976. He fought many battles against rival kings in Leinster and Connacht. The Vikings who had settled in the country often joined forces with local kings and fought for them. This was especially the case around Dublin where the Viking settlers fought Brian Boru fiercely. In 1002, Brian had defeated enough of his enemies to call himself High King of Ireland.

Ulster gave Brian a very hard time. The O'Neills were the ruling family in Ulster and had been for centuries. They were very independent and fought fiercely to keep control of their lands. It took more than ten years for Brian to subdue Ulster and to do it he needed the support of nearly all the kingdoms he had previously conquered.

Brian was generous to the Irish monasteries. In 1005 he gave twenty-two ounces of gold to the monastery at Armagh and declared that Armagh was the religious capital of Ireland. This meant that it was in the interests of Armagh – which is in Ulster – to support Brian. A 9th century manuscript, *The Book of Armagh,* describes Brian as 'the Emperor of the Irish'.

This picture of the Battle of Clontarf was painted in 1826 by Hugh Frazer.

There was one final battle with the Vikings and their Irish allies. It happened in 1014, at **Clontarf**, near Dublin. This is regarded as the greatest battle ever on Irish soil and it was very fierce. They fought all day and thousands were killed on both sides. Eventually Brian Boru's men won and many of the Vikings were driven into the sea where they drowned.

Brian didn't enjoy the victory for very long. He was an old man by this time and had gone back to his tent to pray after the battle. Here is an account of what happened (Earl Brodar and the two warriors with him were Viking survivors):

> *"The attendant perceived a party of the foreigners approaching them. The Earl Brodar was there, and two warriors along with him. 'There are people coming towards us here,' said the attendant.*
>
> *'Alas!' said Brian, 'they are foreigners of the armour, and it is not to do good to thee they come.'*
>
> *While he was saying this, he arose and stepped off the cushion, and unsheathed his sword. Brodar passed him by and noticed him not. One of the three who were there, and who had been in Brian's service, said, 'This is the King.'*
>
> *'No, no, but Priest, Priest,' said Brodar 'It is not he but a noble Priest.'*
>
> *'By no means,' said the soldier, 'that is the great King, Brian.'*
>
> *Brodar then turned round, and appeared with a bright, gleaming, trusty battle-axe in his hand, with the handle set in the middle of it.*
>
> *When Brian saw him, he gazed at him, and gave him a stroke with his sword, and cut off his left leg at the knee, and his right leg at the foot. The foreigner dealt Brian a stroke which cleft his head utterly; and Brian killed the second man that was with Brodar, and they fell both mutually by each other."*

Adapted from *Wars of the Gaedhil with the Gaill*, Rev James H Todd, D.D. London, 1867

**CLEFT:** cut through

## ACTIVITY

In class, role play the death of Brian Boru.

Although Brian did not live to see it, he had finally ended the years of Viking raids in Ireland. After Clontarf, the Vikings retreated to their coastal settlements and did not challenge the kings of Ireland again. Over the years, they integrated into Irish society and culture.

Brian Boru was buried at St Patrick's Church of Ireland Cathedral, Armagh.

**INTEGRATED:** became part of; joined together

THE EARLY MIDDLE AGES

# UNIT 12: THE REST OF THE WORLD

## THE REST OF THE WORLD

Although we have been looking at Britain and Ireland during the Early Middle Ages, there was plenty going on in the rest of the world too.

In central America the Maya civilisation flourished at this time, long before any Europeans had discovered America. The Maya were the most advanced civilisation that had yet developed in the Americas, with a written language, art, fine architecture and mathematics. You can see an example of some Mayan art in the picture on the left.

The Maya built many cities and archaeologists can study their ruins to find out more about the people who lived there. They wrote inscriptions on stones using hieroglyphics (a series of pictures), and historians have been able to translate them. Most are about the Mayan kings and the battles they won.

The civilisation collapsed around 900, but historians are not sure why. It may have been due to climate change, a drought or disease. Although the civilisation collapsed, there are still people who call themselves Maya living there today.

Can you think of any other reasons why a whole civilisation might collapse? What dangers to civilisation are there today that the Mayans did not face?

### ACTIVITY

The Mayan civilisation was situated in an area of central America that is now called the Yucatán Peninsula. Use a map to find it. What country is it in today? Is it closer to the equator than Ireland, or further away? What is the climate like there?

The picture is of a Maya stone carving. It shows U Pakal K'inich who became a Maya King around 740. How useful do you think carvings like this are to historians studying the Maya? Explain why you think this.

In 982, a Viking called Eric the Red, originally from Norway, sailed west and discovered Greenland and brought settlers there from Iceland. His son, Leif Erikson, who was born in Iceland, sailed west from Greenland and in the year 1000 was the first European to set foot in North America. Leif Erikson had brought Christian missionaries with him and they built the first Christian church on the North American continent.

TPD

Today there is a statue of Leif Erikson in the centre of Reykjavik, the capital of Iceland. Why do you think the Icelanders would want to celebrate this man in particular?

In the early 11th century, around the time Brian Boru was fighting the Battle of Clontarf, a Japanese noblewoman called Murasaki Shikibu wrote *The Tale of Gengi*. Some scholars regard this as the world's first novel.

THE EARLY MIDDLE AGES RESEARCH TASK

# UNIT 13: KING ALFRED

WO

You have not yet learnt about the most famous king of all who lived in the Early Middle Ages! He was called **King Alfred.** You must find out all about him yourself.

Form into groups of about four or five. Your task is to investigate the life and achievements of King Alfred. You must present your findings in the way that you feel will best suit you. You may choose one of the following methods:

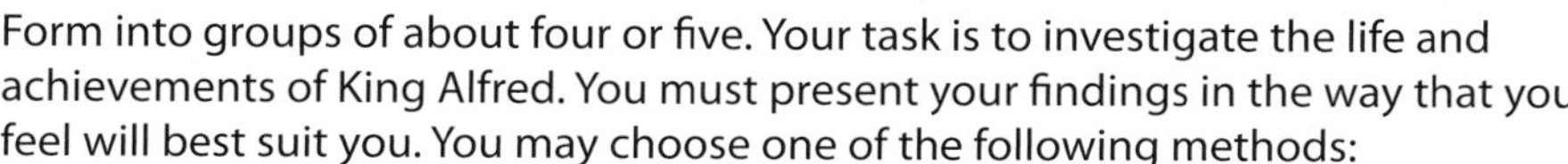

- A talk by one member of your group
- A PowerPoint presentation
- A carefully formatted, word processed biography
- A storyboard with captions. These could be displayed in the classroom and members of your group could explain what each illustration means.

The *minimum* information which you must find out is:

- Alfred's dates of birth and death
- In what Kingdom he was born
- The name of his father and mother
- Who his main opponents were
- His connection with burnt cakes
- What the Danelaw was
- Who wrote a biography of Alfred in 893
- What very important record he ordered to be started
- Alfred's social interests and achievements

In your conclusion you must evaluate King Alfred's reign. Was he a good king, a bad king, or a bit of both?

You must also keep a note of where you found your information – your sources. Add this at the end of your report or, if you created a storyboard, pin this up beside it on a separate sheet.

When all the groups have finished and presented their findings, you should know King Alfred well. Have a class discussion on whether you think you would have liked to meet him.

If you could meet him what would you like to ask him?

Do you think you would have liked to live in King Alfred's Britain? Why or why not?

## Review your work

Did your group find this task interesting?

Did you personally enjoy the task? Why or why not?

Was any part of it particularly difficult?

Did you like working in the group or would you prefer to work on your own?

Was there anything you think your group could have done better? If so, how could it be done better?

# END OF SECTION QUIZ

## Class Quiz!

Divide into two teams and decide on a prize for the winning team. If you get a question right, your team gets a point, BUT if you get a question wrong, you lose a point! So think carefully before you answer.

1. What is the French name for England?
2. Who built the first church at Canterbury?
3. Who won the Battle of Clontarf?
4. Where did the Venerable Bede live?
5. Name two things that were found at Sutton Hoo.
6. Did the Anglo-Saxons have slaves?
7. What did King Canute do at the seaside?
8. Name one thing an Irish round tower may have been for.
9. By what name was the most powerful Irish king known?
10. What country did Eric the Red discover?
11. In what year did the Vikings attack the monastery at Lindisfarne?
12. What important Anglo-Saxon burial was found in Suffolk?
13. What family ruled Ulster at the time of Brian Boru?
14. How did the Anglo-Saxons sweeten their food?
15. Lots of Anglo-Saxons settled in Ireland. True or false?
16. What are the Ides of March?
17. Name two Anglo-Saxon gods.
18. Name three Anglo-Saxon Kingdoms.
19. Why did the Anglo-Saxons keep sheep?
20. Name three Viking settlements in Ireland.

## Word Check

Check out these words to make sure you can spell them.

**venerable**
**Europe**
**hierarchy**
**Northumberland**
**reconstruction**
**lyre**
**poetry**
**burial**
**peasant**
**historian**
**Augustine**
**Canterbury**
**Sutton Hoo**
**archaeologist**
**ecclesiastical**
**ceremony**
**Lindisfarne**
**achievement**
**foreigner**
**opponent**

If you're not sure if you can spell any of them, check them out a few more times.

## Review this Section

So what do you think of the Early Middle Ages?
Share with the class things that you found particularly interesting.
Was there anything that surprised you?
Is there anything more you would like to know? If so, how would you find out about it?

# THE HIGH MIDDLE AGES
# UNIT 14: WHO WERE THE NORMANS?

## THE ORIGIN OF THE NORMANS

Now it's time to have a look at the Normans.

You have probably heard of the Normans before. Write down all you think you know about them: where they came from, what they were like, what they did, and so on.

Keep what you have written somewhere safe and we'll look at it again later.

So who were they?

The word 'Norman' means 'Northman' or 'man from the north'. Today 'Norman' is an ordinary first name and sometimes it's a surname.

Historians believe that the Normans were descended from Viking pirates who settled in northern France in the 9th century. In 911 Charles III, King of France, came to terms with them by granting **Rollo** (the Norman leader, 846–932) the right to rule upper Normandy, probably in return for the Normans becoming Christian and giving Charles III military help.

*Rollo's nickname was 'Rollo the Ganger'. Ganger means 'Walker'. It was said that he was so big and tall that no horse could carry him so he had to walk everywhere!*

However, not everyone who lived in Normandy was Viking. By the time the Normans invaded England in 1066 they had intermarried with the local population and were as much French as they were Viking.

This statue of Rollo is in the town of Falaise in Normandy. 'Rollon' is the French version of Rollo.

## ACTIVITY

Find Normandy on a map.

What are the names of the main towns and cities there today?

# WHAT WERE THE NORMANS LIKE?

We can learn something of what the Normans were like by looking at what modern historians say about them, and at the comments made about them by writers at the time. Two people who wrote about this time were Dudo and William of Malmesbury.

Here are some facts about **Dudo**:

- He was employed by the Norman court to write their history, *The Manners and Deeds of the First Dukes of Normandy*.
- He wrote in (not very good) Latin.
- Historians know that he was not always accurate in his accounts.
- His writings are the only source we have for some of the events he describes.
- He wrote his history about 100 years after the events.

*Dudo wrote with passion. Here is Dudo's description of a man he doesn't like! Perhaps someone could read this out in class.*

> *"This accursed and headstrong, extremely cruel and harsh, destructive, troublesome, wild, ferocious, infamous, destructive and inconstant, brash, conceited and lawless, death-dealing, rude, everywhere on guard, rebellious traitor and kindler of evil, this double-faced hypocrite and ungodly, arrogant, seductive and foolhardy deceiver, this lewd, unbridled, contentious rascal aggravates towards the starry height of heaven an increase of destructive evil and an augmentation of deceit – He is more monstrous than all the rest."*

Here are some facts about **William of Malmesbury** (1095–1145)

- His father was a Norman and his mother was English.
- He was a monk.
- He has been regarded by many as the greatest man of learning in Western Europe in the 12th century.
- He admired the work of the Venerable Bede and modelled his work, *Deeds of the Kings of the English*, on Bede's own work.
- *Deeds of the Kings of the English* was an account of the years 449–1127.
- He wrote in good Latin.
- He is the best source for the history of 12th century England.

## ACTIVITY

Read the following extracts and note who wrote them.
Then answer the questions that follow.

> *In 1066 the Normans, as they are now, were very fussy about their clothes and enjoyed their food, but they were not greedy. They are so used to war that they can hardly live without it.*

William of Malmesbury
*Deeds of the Kings of the English, 1125*

> *These [Normans] certainly cultivated a sense of identity and common characteristics which … tended to be of a military and political type. Ferocity, boundless energy, cunning, and a capacity for leadership were their heritage, to which modern scholars would add supreme adaptability and a simple piety.*

D Nicolle and A McBride
*The Normans, 1987*

**FRANKISH: French**

> *The Frankish bishops said "Anyone who received such a gift ought to bend down and kiss the King's foot". But Rollo said "Never will I bend my knees to anyone, nor will I kiss anyone's foot". But the Franks insisted, so Rollo ordered a certain soldier to kiss the King's foot. The soldier immediately took hold of the King's foot, lifted it up to his mouth and kissed it without kneeling down, so that the King was toppled over backwards.*

Dudo
*The Manners and Deeds of the First Dukes of Normandy, written about 1015*

1. How would you decide whether any of these quotations are primary sources?
2. How can you tell that William of Malmesbury is not writing about his own time?
3. Nicolle and McBride use several adjectives to describe the Normans. Make a list of them. Which are the most complimentary to the Normans?
4. What does Dudo's account tell us about the attitude of Rollo and his soldiers?
5. Which of these quotations would you trust most for accuracy? Explain your answer.

## ACTIVITY

Read Dudo's account again. The King referred to is Charles III who granted Rollo land. Imagine you are a soldier in the King's army and were on duty beside the King when this event happened. Write a letter home to your brother telling him what happened, how you felt about it and about Rollo and his people, and what you did when it happened. You have to use the facts that Dudo tells us, but you can make up anything else you like!

# NORMAN CONQUESTS

By the year 1000 the Normans were firmly established in Normandy. During the next century, the Normans began to expand their military power into other parts of France, into the British Isles and even further afield. The maps show the main places they conquered.

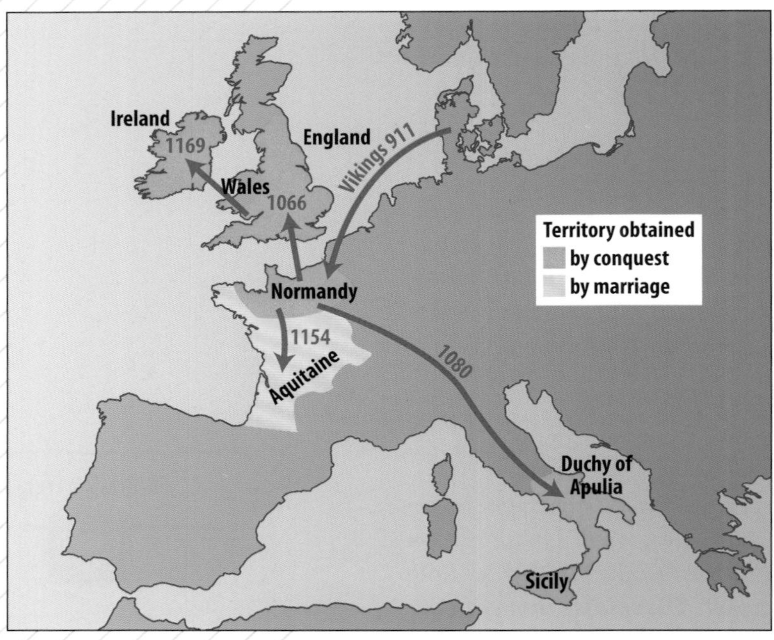


This is a map of Western Europe in the year 1200, showing the areas that the Normans ruled by then, and the years they conquered them.

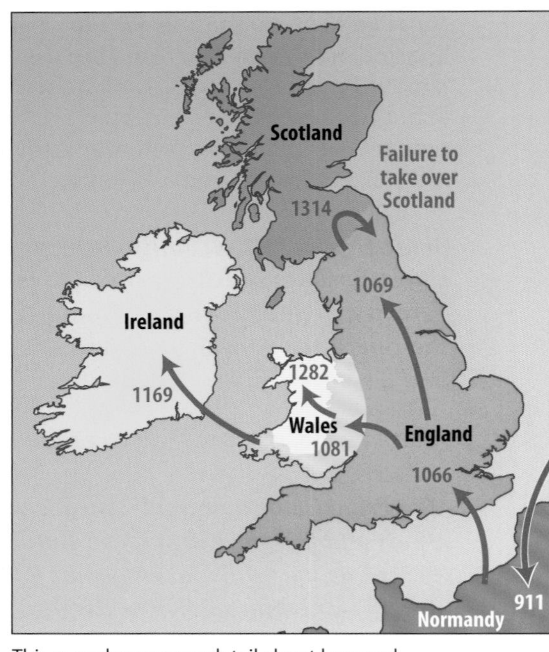


This map shows more detail about how and when the Normans spread their rule over the British Isles.

## ACTIVITY

The Normans conquered the following places:

**England, Ireland, Normandy, Sicily, Wales.**

Write them out in the order in which they were conquered, starting with the earliest.

In the next few units we are going to look in detail at one of the most famous events in English history: the **Norman invasion of 1066**. Until they conquered England in 1066, the Norman leaders were only dukes, and in Normandy itself they continued to be dukes. **William the Conqueror**, whose proper title was **Duke William of Normandy**, led the invasion. After the invasion he also became **King William I** of England – the first Norman to become a king. A century later the Norman armies came to Ireland, and we will be looking at that in more detail.

# UNIT 15: THE BAYEUX TAPESTRY

## SOURCES OF INFORMATION

There are two main sources of information about the Norman conquest of England. You met the first, the Anglo-Saxon Chronicle, in Unit 4. The other is the famous **Bayeux Tapestry**. The Tapestry is a kind of cartoon strip picture story about William coming to England and fighting the Battle of Hastings in 1066. A proper tapestry has the picture actually woven into it, so the Bayeux Tapestry is really an embroidery, not a tapestry.

Here are some facts about the Tapestry:

- It is 50 centimetres high and 70 metres long.
- It is made of linen and embroidered in wool.
- It would stretch across the width of a football pitch.
- In the Tapestry the Normans are called Franci (French).
- It shows 600 men, 200 horses, 50 dogs – and three women!
- Anglo-Saxons are always shown with moustaches.
- Normans are shown with the back of their hair cut short.

## ACTIVITY

Measure the width of your classroom.

If W = width of the classroom and B = the length of the Bayeux Tapestry, solve this equation:

X = B ÷ W. What does the value of X represent?

## COMPARING THE TAPESTRY AND THE CHRONICLE

Historians can learn more about this time by comparing how the same events are recorded in the Anglo-Saxon Chronicle and the Bayeux Tapestry.

### THE COMET

**Halley's Comet** was seen in the sky shortly before the conquest. The comet appears about every 76 years. It last appeared in 1986 and it won't be back until 2061. At the time people did not know what comets were, and so they thought that it must be a sign from God that terrible things were going to happen.

This is how the comet appears on the Bayeux Tapestry. The Latin words at the top translate as 'Here is the wondrous star'.

This is what the Anglo-Saxon Chronicle said of the same event:

> *It happened that all through England such a sign in the heavens was seen as no man had seen before. Some men said that it was the star 'Comet', that some men called the long-haired star. It appeared first on the eve of April 14th, and so shone all seven nights.*

## ACTIVITY

Compare the Tapestry portrayal of the comet with the account in the Anglo-Saxon Chronicle.

What does the Tapestry tell us about it?

What does the Chronicle tell us about it?

What can we learn from the Chronicle that the Tapestry does not tell us?

What do *both* sources tell us?

## ACTIVITY

Imagine you are an English monk living in 1066. You have just seen the comet and you have gone to tell the Abbott (leader) of your monastery about it. Compose a description that you will use to tell him what has happened. Remember that he will be hard to persuade that you were not just seeing things!

**HOLY RELICS: items such as pieces of bone from past saints**

## HAROLD IN NORMANDY

The Tapestry is regarded as the **Norman** version of what happened in 1066, and the Anglo-Saxon Chronicle is regarded as the **Anglo-Saxon** version. The Tapestry uses over a third of its length (25 metres) to explain how an Anglo-Saxon nobleman, Harold, is sent to Normandy by the Anglo-Saxon King, Edward the Confessor; how he is captured by a nasty man called Count Guy of Ponthieu; how William rescues him, treats him well, goes campaigning with him and eventually Harold promises, with his hands on holy relics, to support William's claim to be King of England.

In contrast, one of the Anglo-Saxon Chronicles mentions that Harold went to Normandy, but does not say what he went for.

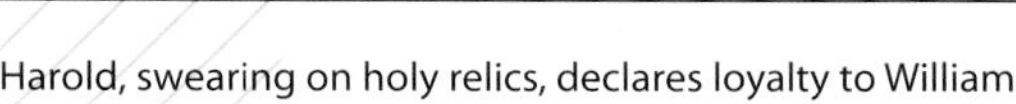

Harold, swearing on holy relics, declares loyalty to William.

Some experts claim that those who embroidered the Tapestry have made Harold appear to be touching the relics reluctantly or with only a finger. Explain why they may think this.

This part of the Tapestry shows William and his nobles having a feast in the open air.

## MAKING THE TAPESTRY

William had a half-brother, Odo. He was the Duke of Kent, as well as Bishop of Bayeux. He commissioned and paid for the Tapestry, and it was probably made to hang at the consecration of Bayeux Cathedral in 1077.

It is now accepted that Odo had the Tapestry embroidered in England, probably Kent. The English were renowned experts in tapestry making.

An expert on the Tapestry, Dr JB McNulty, thinks that the Tapestry gives Bishop Odo's version of events in 1066, not William's. In 1992 he said, "Above all it is to be remembered that it is a work in praise of Bishop Odo's part in the conquest... He appears four times in the Tapestry and every time, he steals the scene."

The nave of Bayeux Cathedral, Normandy, in 1990. Did the Tapestry once decorate each side of it?

Is Odo (holding the club) coming to William's rescue?

In 1992, Professor Francis Neveux, said this about Odo, "He became a Bishop at the age of 20. He had no religious vocation. Youngest sons often went into the church. He had always dreamt of being a ... knight. On the Tapestry you see him holding a club, not a sword. Priests couldn't spill blood. They could only batter their enemies to death."

## ACTIVITY

### Extended writing

Write about 300 words under the title of 'The Bayeux Tapestry'. You want to send this piece to a monthly magazine that specialises in short articles about historical artifacts. Remember to think about who the readers will be, the type of the magazine etc, and write your article to suit it. Word process your article neatly.

## ACTIVITY

You are a journalist working at a daily newspaper in Bayeux today. Your editor has just told you of a major find in the city – a one thousand year old casket has just been dug up at a building site. One of the builders opened it and found that it contains a very long piece of cloth with pictures embroidered on it. The curators of the local museum are on their way to take it away for examination and safe-keeping.

Your editor tells you to get round to the building site quickly. You have about an hour and a half to get the facts, interviews, photographs and a front-page article written before the paper has to go to press.

How do you organise this task? Write an account of what you did to get the article, starting from leaving the office.

Write your article and e-mail it, as an attachment, to another person in the class.

## ACTIVITY

### Making a Plan of Action

Work in pairs for this activity.

Bishop Odo has just commissioned you to organise the creation of what will become the Bayeux Tapestry. Think about all that will need to be organised and jot down all that needs to be done. For example, how much cloth will be needed and how will you get it? Where will the money come from? Don't worry about putting things in order at this stage.

Once you have thought of all you can, look at your list and sort it into the order in which things will need to be done. Put a '1' beside the first thing, '2' beside the second and so on.

When you have done this, take a new page and write at the top: "Plan of Action for the creation of the Bayeux Tapestry". Write out a Plan of Action which is to be taken to Bishop Odo for approval.

# UNIT 16: ENGLAND BEFORE THE NORMANS

## HAROLD BECOMES KING

Let's look at the situation in England just before the Normans invaded. **Edward the Confessor,** (king from 1042–1066) was the son of the previous Anglo-Saxon king, Ethelred II.

He had lived in exile in Normandy from boyhood to middle age. His mother Emma had been Norman, and by the time Edward came to England as king he spoke French, loved Norman things and dressed like a Norman. He was also very religious, which is how he got his nickname, **The Confessor.** He had been brought up by Norman monks and spent a lot of his time building new churches, like Westminster Abbey.

Edward the Confessor

## RESEARCH

Find out about **Westminster Abbey**, London.

A monastery was founded by Dunstan on the site of Westminster Abbey in 960.

Form into groups of five or six and research the history of the Abbey. Your group should compile a list of bullet points, each point giving one interesting fact about it. Try to find at least ten.

When you have finished, the bullet points from all the groups should be compiled into one list. Delete all facts that are duplicated.

Now divide all the facts into separate categories. For example, you could have a category called 'Architecture'. You could have a category called 'People' such as Dunstan and Edward the Confessor.

How many categories can you divide the facts into? Are some facts listed in two or more categories?

Edward the Confessor died in January 1066 but, although he married an Anglo-Saxon, he had no sons to succeed him. You learned in the previous unit how Duke William of Normandy had helped one of England's most powerful noblemen, Harold Godwin. William believed that Harold had promised to support his claim to become King after Edward the Confessor had died. However, Harold was crowned king instead. Here is how the Anglo-Saxon chronicle related this:

> *A.D. 1066. In this year was consecrated the minster at Westminster, on Childermass-day. And King Edward died on the eve of Twelfth-day; and he was buried on Twelfth-day within the newly consecrated church at Westminster. And Harold the earl succeeded to the kingdom of England, even as the king had granted it to him, and men also had chosen him thereto; and he was crowned as king on Twelfth-day.*

This is how the Bayeux Tapestry depicts Harold's coronation.

Can you see Harold's name?

See if you can pick out the objects Harold had been given to identify him as king – the sceptre (a long ornamented stick), the sword of state (representing justice), the crown, and the orb (globe with a cross on top).

Suggest what the orb might represent.

## HAROLD'S REIGN

There are two more sources that tell us about Harold's brief reign as King of England.

**Ordericus Vitalis** lived from about 1075–1142. His mother was English and his father was Norman, and he was born in England. He was proud of being born in England because sometimes he wrote after his name: "Orderic Vitalis Angligena" or "English-born". He wrote many books, several of which have survived. From an historian's point of view, the most important is his *Historia Ecclesiastica (Ecclesiastical History),* which chronicles the history of Normandy and England under the Normans. It consists of thirteen sections, which took Ordericus from about 1109 to 1141 to write. Not all writing was a pleasure. Ordericus wrote, "Worn out with age and infirmity, I long to bring this book to an end". He died shortly after he finished it.

Ordericus Vitalis is regarded as a very reliable source of information; indeed he lived through many of the events he describes.

**Florence of Worcester** was a monk who lived in Worcester and we know that he died in 1118. He played a part in putting together a World Chronicle, known in Latin as *Chronicon ex chronicis.* This was a history of the world from creation until 1140. The writer who continued the Chronicle after Florence died recorded Florence's death in 1118 like this:

*"On 7 July, the Worcester monk Florence died. His meticulous learning and scholarly labours have made this chronicle of chronicles [chronicarum chronica] outstanding among all others.*
*His body is covered by earth, his soul searches the skies.*
*There in the sight of God may he reign among the saints for ever. Amen."*

*Being a man called Florence wasn't as odd in the Middle Ages as it seems now. The name is from the Latin* Florentius*; the girl's equivalent was* Florentia. *It became almost exclusively a girl's name in the nineteenth century after Florence Nightingale became famous for her work nursing soldiers in the Crimean War.*

## ACTIVITY

*Harold was guilty of lying, cruelty and wickedness. In the three months he had been king many people had been badly treated. He had no right to be king.*

Ordericus Vitalis
*Ecclesiastical History of England and Normandy*, 1135

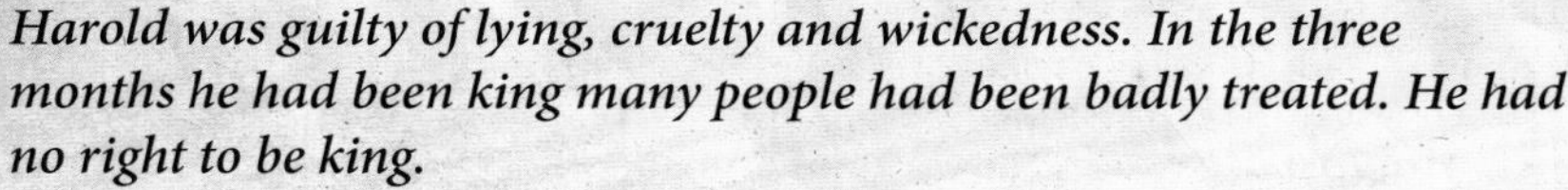

*As soon as Harold became king, he made it his job to stop unfair laws and make good ones. He was kind and polite to all men, but strictly punished all criminals. He ordered the arrest of all thieves and robbers. He worked very hard to defend his country, by land and at sea.*

*Chronicon ex chronicis*, 1130, begun by Florence of Worcester

*1065: yet did the wise king [Edward] entrust his kingdom to a man of high rank, to Harold himself, the noble earl who ever faithfully obeyed his noble lord [King Edward].*

*Anglo-Saxon Chronicle*, 1066

1. Why do you think these writers disagree with each other?
2. Are any of them primary sources? Explain your answer.
3. Should an historian trust one of these sources more than the others?

# UNIT 17: WHO WANTS TO BE KING?

**ATHELING: a prince of a royal dynasty with possible rights to the succession.**

## A DISPUTED THRONE

So Harold had become king, but two other people also thought they should rule England. These were the King of Norway and the Duke of Normandy. A third alternative was Edgar the Atheling, who was still a boy.

Here are some details about them, and the arguments for and against their claim to the throne.

**The King of Norway**

**Name:** Harald Hardrada (Hard Raider)

**Title:** Harald III, King of Norway and Denmark (1047–66)

**For:** He claimed to be the true heir of Canute. Since Canute had ruled England as well as Norway and Denmark, he thought he should too. Harold Godwin's brother Tostig supported him and would supply an army and ships to help dethrone Harold.

**Against:** He was in Norway, not England. Most Englishmen preferred Harold Godwin. Harald wanted more land and more power, and people were very afraid of him. They knew that if Harald invaded England it would renew the old wars between the Danes and the English.

**William of Normandy**

**Name:** William of Normandy

**Title:** Duke of Normandy (since 1035)

**For:** He claimed that Edward the Confessor had promised him the throne of England. Harold had been shipwrecked in 1064 and taken to William in Normandy. William claimed that at that time, Harold had sworn to back him as king, making the oath over holy relics. This was regarded as a very serious act and, by claiming the throne for himself, William felt that Harold was almost committing a crime against him. William was an experienced commander and had good equipment.

**Against:** Harold was already established as king. An invasion of England would require a fleet and could be very risky. He would have little support in England.

### Harold

**Name:** Harold Godwin

**Title:** Harold II, King of England. Previously Earl of Wessex.

**For:** He was the brother-in-law of Edward the Confessor and a good strong fighting leader. He was born and bred in England and was very popular with most of the English. He had been elected King by the Witan (Saxon Council made up of bishops, nobles and advisors). He said that Edward had, on his deathbed, appointed him as his successor. Unfortunately for Harold, there were no witnesses to this.

**Against:** William claimed that Harold had promised to support him as the next king, and had sworn on holy relics to do so.

### Prince Edgar

**Name:** Edgar the Atheling

**Title:** Prince Edgar

**For:** He was the fourteen year old great-grandson of Ethelred the Unready (King of England 978–1013 and 1014–1016). He was also a grand-nephew of Edward the Confessor so he was thus a direct descendant of the Anglo-Saxon royal family; in other words, he was a blood relative of Edward the Confessor. Harold Godwin had only married into it.

**Against:** He was only a boy so could not fight either Duke William or the King of Norway. He had been brought up in Hungary so he had few supporters in England.

## ACTIVITY

Divide into four groups. Each group is supporting one of the four contenders for the throne. In your group, discuss why your contender should be king.

When you have a list of reasons *and understand these reasons,* one person in your group should explain why you think your contender has most right to the throne. When someone from each group has spoken, the floor is open to questions. Anyone can challenge another group about any of their arguments.

Did anyone change their mind? If so, why?

## ACTIVITY

Write a letter from William to his brother Odo (Bishop of Bayeux) in June 1066, explaining why he was going to invade England.

# THE BATTLE OF STAMFORD BRIDGE

Harold thought that William would attack first so he gathered his army in the south of England at London. However, William did not come because, although he had assembled his army and fleet, the wind was against him and he couldn't set sail for England. Instead news came in September that Tostig (Harold's brother) and the King of Norway had landed in Yorkshire. Harold immediately marched north and fought a great battle at Stamford Bridge (25 September 1066).

It was a total victory. Both Tostig and the King of Norway were killed. Three hundred ships had brought 8000 Viking warriors to fight. They needed only twenty four ships to bring the survivors home.

Approximately how many Viking warriors survived to return home?

Here is what Orderic Vitalis wrote about the battle in the early 12th century:

*A hard-fought battle ensued, in which there was great effusion of blood on both sides, vast numbers being slain with brutal rage. At last the furious attacks of the English secured them the victory, and the king of Norway as well as Tostig, with their whole army, were slain. The field of battle may be easily discovered by travellers, as great heaps of the bones of the slain lie there to this day, memorials of the prodigious numbers which fell on both sides.*

# UNIT 18: THE BATTLE OF HASTINGS

## THE NORMANS ARRIVE

Shortly after his victory at Stamford Bridge, messengers reached Harold with news that the wind had changed in William's favour and that he and his army had landed unhindered on the south coast, at **Pevensey.**

Harold immediately marched south, a distance of about 250 miles. His men were exhausted and many of them deserted on the way, to go home and bring in their harvests. Harold did recruit some more men, but they were nearly all peasants with little or no weapons other than pitchforks. Harold arrived near the town of **Hastings** on October 13.

Pevensey Beach where William landed in 1066

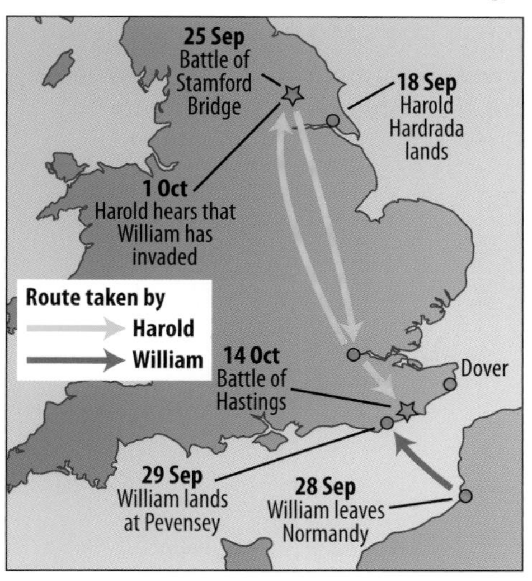


This map shows the long march that Harold and his army had to make to and from Stamford Bridge.

In the time it took Harold to march his army back south again, William had been able to disembark and unload all his horses, archers and men and build two earthwork forts. The next day William and Harold fought each other in battle. It was a long and hard battle but the outcome determined the rest of English history.

**UNHINDERED:** with nothing getting in the way.

**DISEMBARK:** get off or out of, specially a ship.

**INFERIOR:** not as good.

## ACTIVITY

TPD

BC

**Read this description of William arriving in England.**

When Duke William himself landed, as he stepped on the shore he slipped and fell forward upon his two hands. Many of his men raised a loud cry of distress. "An evil sign," they said, "is here." But he cried out lustily: "See, my lords, by the splendor of God, I have taken possession of England with both my hands. It is now mine, and what is mine is yours." This quick thinking and the ability to turn a negative event into a positive one was a major quality that Duke William possessed.

From: www.battle-of-hastings-1066.org.uk/ accessed 28 March 2011

1. If Willam had not thought quickly about what to say when he fell on the beach, what might have happened?
2. Role play the arrival of William and his ships coming in to land and disembarking on English soil. You could have two versions: one based on what actually happened and one based on what might have happened.

## EQUIPMENT

Here are some useful facts about the battle that resulted when the two armies met, and the weapons that the soldiers used:

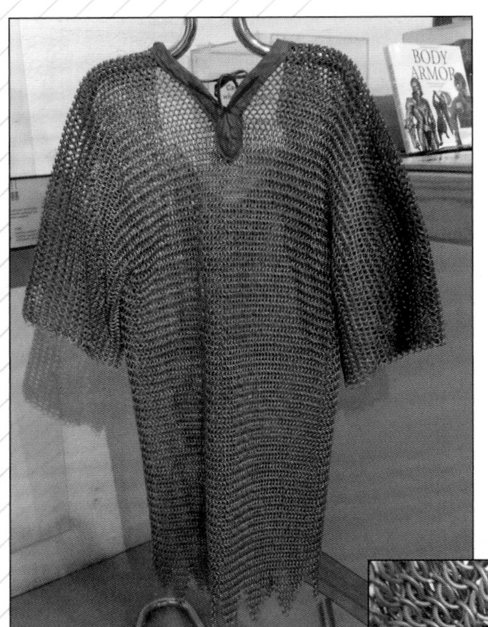

- The Battle was not fought at Hastings at all, but at a place ten kilometres away, now called **Battle.**
- Harold's men were drawn up on a hill called Senlac.
- There were probably 5000-7000 men in each army.
- The battle began at 9.00 am and lasted until dusk, with no break for lunch or tea.
- Both Norman knights and English soldiers wore chain mail and the fashionable conical helmets with a nose piece.
- Their shields were kite shaped, not round.
- Both armies had large numbers of half-armoured men with inferior weapons.
- The Norman archers used short bows, about 1.2 metres in length.
- An archer could kill a man wearing armour 50 metres away. If the man wasn't wearing armour, the archer could kill him from 100 metres away.

This is an example of a chain mail tunic, which soldiers wore for protection. In the second photograph you can see how the chains are linked together. After a battle there might be holes or bent links in the tunic and these would have to be repaired by a blacksmith.

TPD

What do you think it would be like to wear one of these?

## THE BATTLE

**William of Poitiers** was a Norman who wrote a biography of William the Conqueror, *Gesta Guillelmi II ducis Normannorum*. The beginning and end of this work are lost but fortunately the surviving part covers the years 1047–1068. William of Poitiers came from an important Norman family and became chaplain to Duke William. His writing is very biased towards William and the Normans, but he was able to talk to men who had actually taken part in the events he describes, most notably the Battle of Hastings.

Study the following sources on this page and page 66, including the picture.

*Duke William, having intelligence of Harold's approach, ordered his troops to take to their arms on the morning of Saturday. He then heard mass, strengthening both body and soul by partaking of the consecrated host; he also reverently hung from his neck the holy relics on which Harold had sworn.*

Ordericus Vitalis, *Ecclesiastical History of England and Normandy*, 1135

*... braying [blowing] of trumpets announced the outset of battle on both sides. Eager and brave the Normans were first to attack... The English hurled javelins and missiles of all sorts, dealing savage blows with their axes... Then the knights rode forward... they bravely engaged the enemy with their swords. The din of the shouting from the Normans on this side, from the barbarians [English] on that, could hardly be heard for the clash of their weapons and the groans of the dying.*

William of Poitiers, writing about 1071

*The Norman infantry turned in flight... almost the whole battle line of Duke William fell back, a fact which can be admitted without affront [insult] to the Normans... The Normans imagined that their Duke had fallen, but he rushed after his retreating troops, dragged off his helmet and showed his bared head. "Look at me!" he shouted, "I am still alive! With God's help I shall win"... They took new courage from his words and he himself rode on again at their head.*

William of Poitiers

*The English who were so sure of themselves fought with all their might, they were so tightly massed that the men who were killed could hardly fall on the ground. The Normans realised that they could never overcome the vast army of their enemies... They therefore withdrew, pretending to turn in flight. Some thousand or more of the English rushed boldly forward; suddenly the Normans turned their horses, cut off the force which was pursuing them, encircled them and massacred them to the last man. Twice the Normans used this trick with equal success.*

William of Poitiers

*At last the English began to weary. Evening was now falling; they knew that their king with two of his brothers and many other great men had been killed. Those who remained were almost exhausted, and they realised that they could expect no more help.*

*They began to flee as swiftly as they could, some on foot, some along the roads, but most over the trackless countryside. The Normans eagerly carried on the pursuit, and striking the rebels in the back brought a happy end to this famous victory.*

William of Poitiers

*The Normans had two military weapons which the English lacked, namely archers and heavy armed calvary. It was by the skillful and daring use of these that Duke William solved the difficult problem with which he was confronted, and at the end of a hard-fought day won the signal victory at Hastings, the most important in English History.*

Hutchinson's Early History of the British Nations, 1939

*That Hastings was a decisive defeat of infantry by cavalry-with-archers is, of course, a common place of History... The fact was that Harold through his very energy in taking a large force to the north to deal with Hardrada, and then through his impetuosity in returning to meet William before he could deploy all the resources undoubtedly available to him, had greatly weakened his chances of success.*

GWS Barrow, *Feudal Britain,* 1956

This panel on the Bayeux Tapestry shows William's knights charging at the Battle of Hastings.

## ACTIVITY

1. Which of these sources are primary and which are secondary?
2. From the writings of William of Poitiers, pick out four words or phrases that indicate his bias towards William and the Normans.
3. Describe the picture from the Bayeux Tapestry.
    - Do you think there is a sense of speed in the scene? If so, how has this been achieved?
    - Do you see any weak points in the armour of the soldiers and horses?
    - What do you think they are holding up in their right arms?
4. Using all the written sources, write out a list of reasons why William may have won the battle.

## ACTIVITY

Form into groups of four or five. Write a short play about an English peasant who has escaped from the carnage at the Battle of Hastings. He has travelled a long way to get home to his family. They have not seen him since he joined Harold's army as it marched north to fight the Vikings at Stamford Bridge. Everyone in the group must have a part to play.

Through the dialogue, you have to convey to your audience the experience of this man and his friends. Think about:

- How is he feeling physically and emotionally?
- What has he seen?
- Who had he left behind to go and fight for Harold?
- Did he want to go?
- Did others from his village go too? What became of them?
- What is the reaction of his family when he returns?

Act your plays in class and then organise a secret ballot to vote on which was the best. Perhaps the winner could be asked into another history class to perform their play!

# UNIT 19: THE DEATH OF HAROLD

## HAROLD IS DEFEATED

King Harold did not survive the Battle of Hastings. In this unit you will find out what happened.

**Gerald of Wales** (1146–1223) – known in Latin as Geraldus Cambrensis – came from a noble family in Wales. His father was of Norman descent and his mother was Welsh. He was a highly educated clergyman and has been called the "universal scholar" and "one of the most learned men of a learned age". He was very proud of being Welsh and wrote extensively about both Wales and Ireland. He also had a great appreciation of music and his writings give historians insight into the music and instruments of his times.

**Matthew of Westminster** never existed! This name was given by mistake to the author of an English history, *Flores Historiarum* ('Flowers of History'). In fact many of the later writers who contributed to this work lived at Westminster. The *Flores Historiarum* covers the years from Creation to 1326 and is particularly valuable as a source for the years 1215 – 1235. In these later years, the writers were describing events taking place in their own lifetimes.

## THE DEATH OF HAROLD

### ACTIVITY

TPD

Study all the sources on this page and page 68, including the picture, to find out what happened to King Harold.

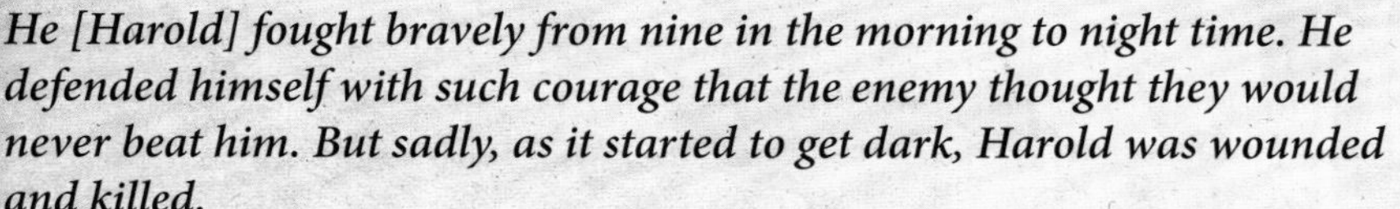

*He [Harold] fought bravely from nine in the morning to night time. He defended himself with such courage that the enemy thought they would never beat him. But sadly, as it started to get dark, Harold was wounded and killed.*

Florence of Worcester, writing about 1116

*At last Harold fell after his brain had been split through by an arrow. But while the king was still breathing, one of the Normans ran up to him and cut off his leg. William had him beaten for this and expelled from the army.*

*He sent the body of King Harold to his mother. William did not want the large ransom that she had offered for his body. When she received it, she buried it at Waltham in the church which Harold himself had built.*

'Matthew of Westminster', writing about 1320

**ANCHORITE: A hermit, someone who lives alone away from ordinary society.**

*He was wounded in many places, losing his left eye through an arrow which went into it. But, although beaten, he escaped to these parts. It is believed that he led the life of an anchorite, passing his days in one of the local churches (until his death). The real identity of [Harold] was only revealed when [he made his] last confession.*

Gerald of Wales, writing in 1188

*Harold had no badges on him and could not be identified by his face, only by certain marks on his body. King William gave it to William Malet for burial, and not to Harold's mother. She wanted to bury Harold herself and offered William her son's weight in gold. But the King thought that it was wrong to get money in this way. He did not think Harold should be buried as his mother wanted, because so many men had died because of his greed. He said jokingly that, because Harold had tried so hard to guard the coast of England, he should be buried by the sea shore.*

William of Poitiers, writing about 1071

1. The Battle of Hastings was fought in 1066. Calculate the number of years after the event that each of the sources was written or created. (If you have forgotten the date of the Bayeux Tapestry, check it out in Unit 15. List them in chronological order starting with the earliest.
2. Make two lists. In one, list the facts on which all these sources agree. In your second list, write all the facts on which these sources disagree. Which is the longer list? What factors may account for the differences between them?
3. Decide which of these sources you feel is most trustworthy for an historian. Remember to take into account what you know about each of the writers and the Bayeux Tapestry. Write about 100 words explaining the reasons for your choice.
4. Look at the picture of the Bayeux Tapestry. The words at the top read 'Harold rex interfectus est', which means 'Here King Harold has been killed'. The name 'Harold' is written above a warrior with an arrow in his eye. The words 'interfectus est' (has been killed) are above a second warrior being hacked down by a Norman soldier on horseback. Discuss which one you think is Harold.

## ACTIVITY

Design and colour your own Battle of Hastings battle scene. Put your drawings up as a display in the classroom.

# AFTER THE BATTLE

**Edith Swan-Neck** had been the consort (wife) of Harold for over twenty years at the time of his death. Because Harold's body was mutilated by Norman soldiers, he could not be identified on the battlefield. Edith Swan-Neck walked through all the carnage of dead bodies in order to find him. She said she would know him by marks on his chest. This is a picture showing how one artist imagined the moment she found him.

TPD

Talk about this picture in class.

1. Do you think it is probable that this is an accurate representation of what happened that day? Why or why not?
2. What words would you use to describe the mood of this picture?
3. What clue is there to show that Norman soldiers died as well as English soldiers?
4. Who are the two men with Edith and why do you think they are with her?

COM TPD WO

## ACTIVITY

### Hot Seat

Pick two people to sit at the front, facing the class. One will play the part of Harold and the other will be William.

The rest of the class can ask them questions and they must answer them. Think up your own questions but here are two examples of what you might ask:

"Harold, why did you march to fight William's army when your men were all so tired from fighting at Stamford Bridge?"

"William, were you surprised that there was no-one to challenge you when you landed in England?"

BC

## ACTIVITY

### Extended writing

Write about the Norman invasion in your own words. Call it *either* "Why William Won" *or* "Why Harold Lost". You might like to include:

- William's landing at Pevensey
- Harold's march south
- Description of the fighting
- Harold's death
- William's victory

Don't just describe the events. Try also to write about why they won or lost.

THE HIGH MIDDLE AGES

# UNIT 20: THE NORMANS CONQUER ENGLAND

## WILLIAM BECOMES KING

The Battle of Hastings did not immediately make William King of England. William waited five days but no one came to offer him the crown. Then he marched along the coast to Dover and burnt the castle. This scared the people of Canterbury and when William neared their town they immediately surrendered.

Meanwhile in London all was confusion. Some wanted to fight on and make Prince Edgar king (see Unit 17). Others thought William should be offered the crown.

William passed London along the south bank of the Thames, crossed the river at Wallingford and approached London from the west. At this time the city was only on the north bank of the river. At Berkhamsted the chief earls and bishops, as well as Edgar, met him and accepted William as King.

South-eastern England showing William's route from Hastings to London.

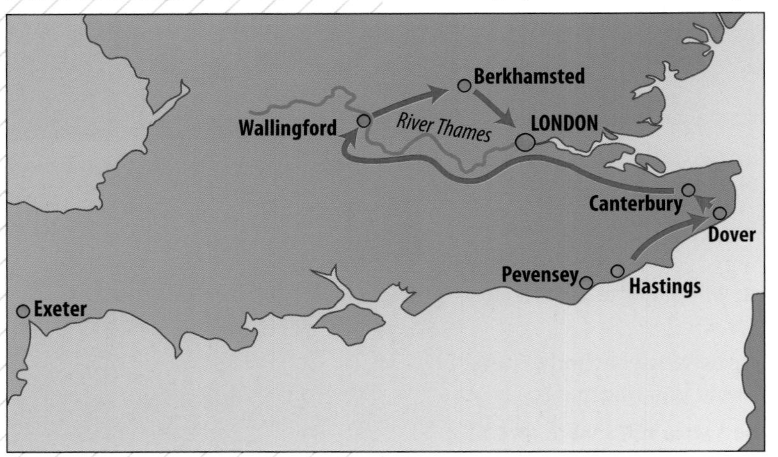


He was crowned on **Christmas Day 1066** at Westminster Abbey. William did not execute Prince Edgar. Edgar became involved in a rebellion in the north of England. He outlived William and died in 1125.

London had accepted William as King but not all of the country agreed! In 1068 the people of Exeter refused to admit William to the city and a siege followed. William soon took the city and built a castle there. William gave his barons land which he had confiscated and instructed them to build castles on this land also. Most of these early castles were wooden.

Q

Read this extract:

> *With God's help, the king easily conquered the city of Exeter when it rebelled. Part of the wall fell down accidentally and this made an opening for him. He attacked it very fiercely because one of the men standing on the wall had bared his bottom and broken wind in front of the Normans.*
>
> William of Malmesbury, writing about 1125.

Why do you think this incident annoyed William so much?

What does William's response to this gesture tell you about him?

# THE HARRYING OF THE NORTH

In 1069 Sweyn, the new King of Denmark, sent 300 ships to the north of England. William marched north but the Danes returned to their ships and played cat and mouse with William for a week before sailing home.

In 1070 William took his revenge on the people of the north who had supported the Danes. He burnt their crops, destroyed their villages and probably caused a famine that killed thousands. This is known as the **Harrying of the North**.

**HARRYING:** annoying, causing suffering through constant agitation.

**HUSBANDRY:** farming, specially growing crops and keeping animals for food.

**IMPLEMENTS:** tools.

Not much is known about **Henry of Huntingdon** (about 1080–1160). He was Archdeacon of Huntingdon and his most famous work is *Historia Anglorum* (History of the English). This account finishes in 1154 and it is likely that Henry died shortly after this.

Read these two accounts of the Harrying of the North.

*In the whole country there was a famine. People were so hungry that they ate human flesh, as well as horses, dogs and cats. Some people became slaves to try to stay alive. Others left their country, but fell down in the middle of the journey and died.*

*It was horrific to see human corpses decaying in the houses and roads, and swarming with worms. There was a terrible smell, because no one was left to bury them, all having been killed by the sword or by the famine.*

*For nine years, no one lived in the villages between York and Durham. They became places where wild animals and robbers lurked, and they were a great danger to travellers.*

Henry of Huntingdon, writing about 1120

*Never did William commit so much cruelty, to his lasting disgrace, he yielded to his worst impulse and set no bounds to his fury condemning the innocent and the guilty to a common fate. In the fullness of his wrath he ordered the corn and cattle with the implements of husbandry and every sort of provisions to be collected in heaps and set on fire till the whole was consumed and thus destroyed at once all that could serve for the support of life in the whole country lying beyond the Humber...in a Christian nation more than a hundred thousand souls of both sexes and all ages perished.*

Orderic Vitalis

## ACTIVITY

### Class debate

Organise a class debate on the motion: "This house believes that William the Conqueror was wrong to react to the northern rebellion in the way that he did."

THE HIGH MIDDLE AGES **CASE STUDY**

# UNIT 21: HEREWARD THE WAKE

A drawing showing Hereward surviving an ambush.

One of the last places to resist William was the fenlands of Cambridgeshire. In 1071 this area consisted of miles of swamps and small islands. It was here that a colourful local character called **Hereward the Wake** used the Isle of Ely as a base from which to raid Norman farms and villages. Many stories were told about him, most of them legend. His sword was called Brainbiter.

In 1071 William sent an army to crush Hereward by building a causeway to the Isle of Ely. However, the causeway collapsed and many soldiers drowned.

It was rumoured that Hereward had used black magic to destroy the causeway. William built a tower and put a witch in it to cast a spell on Hereward, but Hereward's men burnt the tower and the witch. At last William found a secret route to the island and captured it. But Hereward the Wake escaped and it is not known where he went.

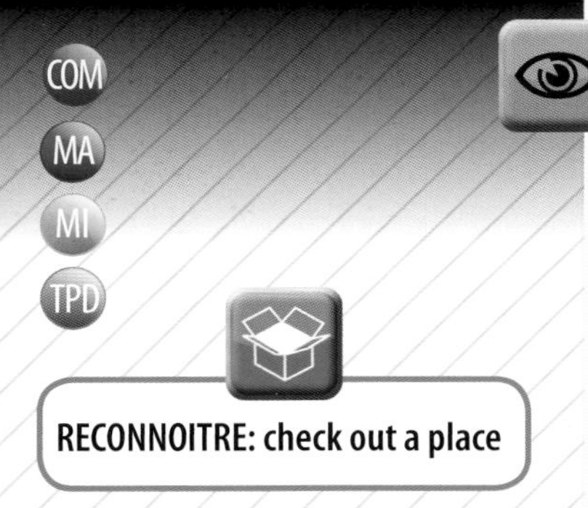


RECONNOITRE: check out a place

## RESEARCH

The city of Ely now exists at this location. Use an atlas to find out where the city of Ely is. What are its latitude and longitude (to the nearest degree)?

Research what the Isle of Ely was like at the time of Hereward the Wake.

You are a soldier in the army of William the Conquerer and he has sent you to reconnoitre the Isle of Ely. You have to present him with a full report on the area and what it would be like to fight on this terrain.

Give William advice on the best way to defeat Hereward.

## ACTIVITY

From Hereward's point of view, what advantages and disadvantages does he have in hiding in the Isle of Ely?

## ACTIVITY

Draw a picture of the witch in the tower.

# UNIT 22: WILLIAM AS KING

## THE DOMESDAY BOOK

William decided that he wanted to know about everything that people owned in the country that he had conquered. By having an accurate picture of this, he could collect all the taxes due to him. Here is the entry in the Anglo-Saxon Chronicle:

> ***"While spending the Christmas of 1085 in Gloucester, William had deep speech with his counsellors and sent men all over England to each shire to find out what or how much each landholder had in land and livestock, and what it was worth. …So very narrowly, indeed, did he commission them to trace it out, that there was not one single hide, nor a yard of land, nay, moreover (it is shameful to tell, though he thought it no shame to do it), not even an ox, nor a cow, nor a swine was there left, that was not set down in his writ."***

**HIDE: a measurement of land, between 60 and 120 acres.**

Once something was written down in the Domesday (pronounced 'Doomsday') Book, it became law and there was no appeal against it. So if you thought that you owned a piece of land – or even a chicken – but William's surveyors decided it belonged to someone else, you had lost it. Because of this, people at the time said the Book had the same authority as the Final Day of Judgement, in other words – Domesday!

A page from the Domesday Book, recording details of land, animals and people in Warwickshire.

Here are some of the questions that were asked by the surveyors:

- How many ploughs are there in the manor?
- How many mills and fishponds?
- How many freemen, villagers and slaves are there in the manor?
- How much woodland, pasture, meadow?
- What does each freeman owe in the manor?
- How much is the manor worth?

Through the Domesday Book, historians can see how certain areas had suffered after the coming of William the Conqueror. For example, in the reign of Edward the Confessor (the king before Harold) there were 1607 houses in York. By the time of the Domesday survey there were only 967 houses in the city.

**MANOR: where a lord lived**

What had happened to York and the surrounding area that might account for its decline?

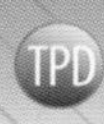

The Domesday Book was written in Latin and was compiled within one year. This was very fast because over 13,418 places are recorded and they didn't have computers in those days!

The Domesday Book is extremely important for historians as a record of 11th century life in England. There is no other document like it in the whole of Europe. It is preserved in the National Archives in London but you can also see some of it online at: www.nationalarchives.gov.uk/documentsonline/domesday.asp

## ACTIVITY

Write a modern Domesday Book for your school. List the questions you would need to ask.

Think about the best way to collect the information.

How would you present your findings?

What things could people in the future find out from your entry?

# THE WHITE TOWER

**FLAGON: a large bottle, often with a spout.**

*The first prisoner in the White Tower was also the first prisoner to escape from it!*

*Ranulf Flambard, a Norman and Bishop of Durham, was imprisoned there in 1100. The story goes that friends smuggled in a rope inside a flagon of wine. Ranulf gave the wine to his jailors and when they were drunk he lowered himself out of his cell window and escaped.*

It took the Normans five years to completely conquer England. The Normans were great castle builders. These were not previously known in England as methods of enforcing rule. Orderic Vitalis wrote:

> *The fortifications called castles by the Normans were scarcely known in England and so the English – in spite of their courage and love of fighting – could put up only weak resistance to their enemies.*

The White Tower

We will study castles in more detail later, but one of the most important Norman Castles is still in use in London. The White Tower was started by William the Conqueror in 1078. Today it is part of the **Tower of London.**

It was built using stone from Caen in France. William had the stone specially imported for the work.

THE HIGH MIDDLE AGES

# UNIT 23: FEUDALISM

## HOW FEUDALISM WORKED

Today most farmers own the land they farm, or else they rent it from someone else for money. In the Middle Ages it didn't work like that. No one *owned* land except the King and the Church. Everyone else *held* their land in exchange for duties and services (not money). If they did not carry out the duties, the land was taken from them. This was called the **Feudal System.**

It worked something like this:

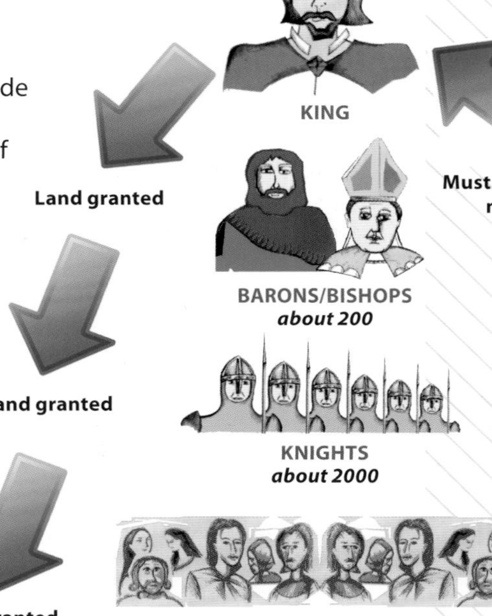

## TYPES OF PEOPLE

### THE KING

The king was the top of the Feudal System. It made it easy for him to control his barons. He granted them a lot of land in return for an oath of fealty. If they rebelled against him the oath was broken and he could take the land back.

### BARONS

Barons had to appear at court, pay taxes to the king and supply 20-30 fully armed knights and about 400 foot soldiers in time of war. Feudalism was how the king got an army. Each baron had land equal to about 500 square kilometres, usually scattered in several places. They in turn gave land to about 20-30 knights in return for an oath of fealty from them.

### KNIGHTS

A knight had to fight for his lord and supply about 20 foot soldiers as well. He also had to supply food and money to the baron. The knight in his turn usually controlled a town or village and got these things from his peasants, who had to be loyal to him. Some knights had no land but hoped to be rewarded with land if they fought well.

### PEASANTS

Peasants (or **villeins**) depend on the knight for their land. They had to be loyal to him, fight for him in time of war, and carry out lots of duties. These activities did not leave a lot of time to work on their own land. The big advantage was that their knight had to protect them if another baron or knight threatened them. They might have to pay taxes to the king. By the Late Middle Ages, many peasants were being paid to work on the lord's land.

DUES: money or other gifts you had to give your lord.

FEALTY: faithfulness or loyalty.

VILLEIN: a peasant who was not a slave.

## THE CHURCH

The king directly owned about a quarter of England (mostly the forests), and the barons about half. The remaining quarter was owned by the Church, mostly by abbeys, and so many villeins worked for an abbot instead of a knight or baron. In return the Church helped the king to run the country, and taught everyone to obey the king and barons.

## ACTIVITY

Read this extract from the Domesday Book:

> *Adam Underwood holds 30 acres of his lord, the Earl of Warwick, and in return he has to give the following dues and services:*
>
> 1. *Work every Monday, Wednesday and Friday from October to August. Work two days a week from August to October. This can be ploughing, haymaking, harvesting, carting stones and gathering nuts.*
> 2. *Leave his own land at haymaking and harvest time and work for his lord.*
> 3. *Make gifts of oats, a hen and food for three horses, 12 pence at Christmas, 1 penny for every pig a year old and a half a penny for younger ones.*

Imagine you are Adam Underwood. Write a diary covering a week during September (harvest time). Describe the activities you carried out for your lord during the week, and on what days. Which days did you work for yourself? Describe the work you think he might have done on those days. Do you think he might have worked harder on some days than on others? Why?

## ACTIVITY

Here is an example of an oath taken in Norman times by anyone who received land from someone:

> *I become your man from this day forward, for life and limb and loyalty. I shall be true and faithful to you for the lands I hold from you.*

Does anything in particular strike you about this oath?

What examples of present-day oaths can you think of?

Why do you think it is necessary to swear oaths?

# UNIT 24: DERMOT OF THE FOREIGNERS

## IRELAND

Let's look now at what was happening in Ireland after the Normans had conquered England. Although England used the feudal system, Ireland was governed by the ancient system of **Brehon Law**. Under Brehon Law the land did not belong to the king, or the chief, but to the whole tribe. Thus even the lowest of the free tribesmen had as much right to his share of land as the chief did. The chief was appointed by the wider clan in a sort of election.

## ACTIVITY

Organise an election for your class, to appoint a class representative. What would you like the representative to be able to do for your class? You will need nominees, ballot papers and independent people to count the votes. Each nominee must say what they would do for the class.

**CONTROVERSIAL: Something that not everyone agrees on and can cause arguments.**

In 1166 the King of Tyrone, who was High King, was overthrown and killed in a rebellion by his sub-kings who then gave their support to Rory O'Connor, King of Connaught. O'Connor then became High King. **Dermot MacMurrough** was the King of Leinster. He is one of the most controversial people in Irish history, because Irish writers called him 'Diarmait na nGall' – meaning he was the man who brought the foreigners to Ireland. In other words he is regarded as responsible for bringing the English into Ireland.

This is not strictly true. Several Norman influences were to be seen in Ireland before the first knights arrived in 1169. Dermot was one of a number of Irish rulers who had begun to copy the fashions of the Normans in clothes and behaviour. In addition, St Malachy, Archbishop of Armagh, had set up Cistercian (French style) abbeys at Mellifont (Co Louth) and Jerpoint (Co Kilkenny).

Here is how Gerald of Wales described Dermot:

> *Dermot was tall and well built, a brave and warlike man among his people, whose voice was hoarse from constantly having been in the din of battle. He was obnoxious to his own people and hated by others. He preferred to be feared than to be loved.*

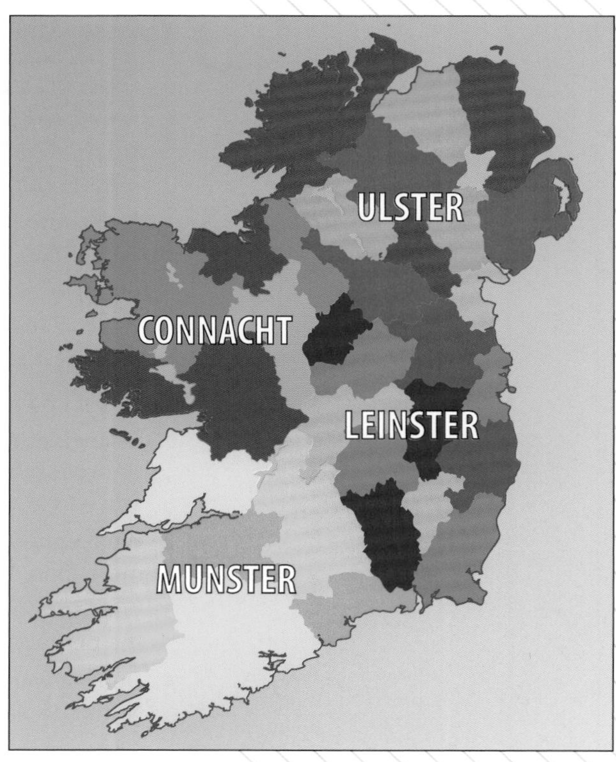


The four provinces of Ireland today, and the counties within them. The names are those of Irish kingdoms that existed before the Normans. Northern Ireland includes 6 of the 9 counties of Ulster.

Who do you think makes the best leader – one who is feared or one who is loved?

Dermot MacMurrough

**MERCENARIES: Soldiers who fight for anyone in return for money.**

# DERMOT AND THE NORMANS

Dermot had hoped to be High King himself one day, but he had much to fear from Rory O'Connor becoming High King. Rory encouraged Dermot's sub-kings in Leinster to desert him. O'Connor invaded Leinster in 1166. Dermot went to his Norman friends in Wales to look for help. Wales had already been occupied by the Normans and the Welsh archers were famous for their skill. What Dermot wanted was to recruit mercenaries to help him recover his kingdom.

Dermot's Norman friends were unwilling to offer help unless Dermot first got the approval of their King, Henry II. Henry was fighting a war in France so Dermot travelled there to see him. Dermot knew the way the feudal system worked (see Unit 23). He swore loyalty to Henry as his overlord, in effect recognising Henry as High King. In return Henry would have to give him protection as a vassal. With letters of support from Henry II, Dermot returned to Wales and recruited a Norman army. This army began to arrive in Ireland in 1169.

One reason Henry II was willing to help was that, in 1155, the Pope (Adrian IV) had given his blessing to Henry II to come to Ireland. This was because the Irish church was not yet under the control of the Pope, so Henry would 'enlarge the boundaries of his [the Pope's] church' by taking control of Ireland. When Dermot came to Henry, he saw this as an opportunity to carry out the Pope's wishes.

This is the letter given by Henry II to Dermot MacMurrough in 1167:

> *Henry, King of England, Duke of Normandy and Aquitaine and Count of Anjou, to all his liegemen, English, Normans, Welsh and Scots, and to all nations subject to his sway sends greetings. Whensoever these our letters shall come to you, know you that we have taken Dermot, prince of the men of Leinster, into the bosom of our grace and good will. Wherefore, too, whosoever within the bounds of our dominions shall be willing to lend aid to him, as being our vassal and liegeman, in the recover of his own, let him know that he has our favour and permission to that end.*

1. Henry's letter to his subjects was hand written, as everything was at that time. How could he make sure that people reading it knew it had come from him and was not a fake?
2. What words or phrases in Henry's letter might make you think that there was more than one letter? Why might there be more than one?
3. Why do you think the Norman lords did not want to fight for Dermot without the permission of the king?
4. Dermot wanted help in getting his lands back from Rory O'Connor. He asked Norman soldiers to fight for him in an internal Irish battle. Is this surprising?

# UNIT 25: THE COMING OF STRONGBOW

## THE NORMANS ARRIVE IN IRELAND

Dermot had gone to seek help in 1166, but it was to be three years before the first Normans arrived, in 1169. Meanwhile O'Connor, the High King, had allowed Dermot to keep a small bit of land near Wexford. It was here that the first Normans landed in May 1169 with fewer than 400 men.

Why did the Normans come to fight for Dermot? Read these comments from one of the Norman lords, called Fitzstephen, who came to Ireland to fight for Dermot.

> *We are restoring the fortunes of this honourable man [Dermot], our excellent and generous benefactor, who has been cheated by the treachery of his own people.*

> *Perhaps the outcome of this present action will be that the five divisions of the island will be reduced to one, and the sovereignty over the whole kingdom will devolve upon our race in the future.*

> *It is not, then, greed for monetary rewards or the 'blind craving for gold' that has brought us to these parts, but a gift of lands and cities in perpetuity to us and to our children.*

**ACTIVITY** Make a mind map of the motives and problems Fitzstephen had to consider in deciding to come to Ireland. Start like this:

TPD

*Fitzstephen: "Shall I go to fight in Ireland?"* — *I would have to leave my English lands.* — *I could leave enough men behind to defend and manage them.*

This first batch of Normans captured Wexford from the Vikings. O'Connor was so impressed by this success that he made peace with Dermot and restored him as King of Leinster. Dermot promised to bring no more foreigners to Ireland, but soon broke his word. Maurice Fitzgerald arrived in August 1169 with more Normans, and in May 1170 **Strongbow** himself arrived.

# STRONGBOW CAPTURES DUBLIN

Richard de Clare (Strongbow) was a very important Welsh Norman. He had lost his land, and Henry II half promised that he could make up for this by getting land in Ireland. He landed in 1170 with a considerable force of 1200 men, 200 of them knights. He and Dermot captured Waterford and then marched north and captured Dublin. Strongbow married Dermot's eldest daughter Aoife (pronounced 'Eefa') and Dermot promised that when he died, Strongbow would become King of Leinster.

The marriage of Strongbow and Aoife, painted in the 19th century.

Dermot now had plans to defeat O'Connor and make himself High King, but he died suddenly in 1171 and Strongbow declared himself King of Leinster.

Dermot MacMurrough was particularly unpopular in Ireland because of his violence towards his own Irish people, but also because he was the first person to invite armies from England and Wales into Ireland to fight the Irish.

Here is what a monk in Donegal wrote, around the year 1171:

> ***Dermot MacMurrough, King of Leinster, by whom a trembling sod was made of all Ireland, after bringing over the Saxons, after having done extensive injury to the Gael, after plundering and burning many churches in Kells, Clonard etc, died at Ferns before the end of the year after this plundering, by an insufferable and unknown disease, through the miracles of God, Columba and Finnan, whose churches he had profaned some time before without will, without penance, without the body of Christ, as his evil deeds deserved.***

## ACTIVITY

Imagine you are an Irish peasant in Leinster. Write two diary entries:

The first, in 1166, explaining why you support Dermot.

The second, in 1171, explaining why you are now angry with him.

O'Connor now realised what a threat Strongbow was so he attempted to recapture Dublin by allying himself with the Vikings from the Isle of Man and the Western Isles of Scotland, as well as all the other Irish Kings.

This army of about 30,000 surrounded Dublin, which was defended by only about 2000 Normans. O'Connor was defeated when the Normans made a surprise attack on the Irish/Viking camp. O'Connor was having a bath in his tent at that moment, and had to make a run for it, presumably still wet! As a result of the battle, Strongbow was further strengthened as King of Leinster.

# UNIT 26: HENRY II COMES TO IRELAND

## WHY DID HENRY COME?

Henry II himself arrived in Ireland in October 1171. Why did he come? Here are some reasons:

1 As early as 1154, when Henry II became king, he had ambitions to add Ireland to the countries he ruled.

2 As we know, Pope Ardian IV had given his blessing to Henry II coming to Ireland in 1155. Incidentally this Pope was an Englishman. Might this have helped? Here is an extract from the Papal Bull *Laudabiliter,* by which the Pope granted Ireland to King Henry II in England in 1155:

> *Adrian, bishop, servant of the servants of God, to our beloved son in Christ the illustrious King of the English, greeting... as becomes a Catholic prince, your purpose to enlarge the boundaries of the church, to proclaim the truths of the Christian religion to a rude and ignorant people... we therefore do declare our will and pleasure that, with a view to enlarging the boundaries of the Church... you shall enter that island and execute* [carry out] *whatsoever may tend to the honour of God and the welfare of that land...*

3 When Dermot came to Henry in 1167, this gave Henry the opportunity he needed to get a foothold in Ireland.

4 By 1171 Henry II was in bad favour with the new Pope (Alexander III) because in 1170 Henry's knights had murdered Thomas Becket, the Archbishop of Canterbury. Henry hoped to make up for this crime by invading Ireland and giving the Pope control over the Irish church.

5 Henry was alarmed and angered by Strongbow taking the title King of Leinster and decided to come to Ireland to show who was boss, so to speak. An historian wrote this in 1197:

> *When these* [Strongbow's] *successes had become known to the King of England, he was moved to anger against the Earl for having attempted so great an enterprise, not only without consulting him but even in defiance of him, and also because the Earl had taken to himself the glory of so noble a conquest, which ought rather to have been given to the King as his superior.*

## HENRY ARRIVES

Strongbow realised that by making himself a king he had gone too far. He met Henry in Wales and made peace with him. He renewed his oath of homage, and handed over all the lands he had conquered. In October 1171 Henry II arrived in Ireland with a considerable force of 250 ships, 500 knights, and up to 4000 archers and foot soldiers.

Both Irish and Normans had good reason to be scared. All the Norman lords submitted to Henry in Dublin. Strongbow was granted Leinster, but as a lord, not a king. Hugh de Lacy was appointed as the King's representative in Ireland. Henry kept Dublin, Wexford and Waterford for himself.

## ACTIVITY

In pairs, write a short scene in which Strongbow meets King Henry. Henry is very angry with Strongbow and Strongbow has to make a case for Henry forgiving him.

The Rock of Cashel, Co Tipperary, where the Kings of Munster were traditionally crowned. The Irish bishops met here in 1172.

The Irish kings deserted Rory O'Connor and rushed to Dublin to recognise Henry II as their lord. Early in 1172 the Irish bishops and abbots met at Cashel, and promised to bring the Irish church into line with the rest of Europe, and to recognise fully the Pope's authority. Henry then returned to England. This helped Henry to make his peace with the Pope. In 1173 Becket was declared a saint (Saint Thomas) and a year later Henry II did penance by walking barefoot through Canterbury, and being whipped by bishops at Becket's tomb.

Henry II never returned to Ireland, but his knights continued to take land from the Irish Kings. De Lacy conquered Meath in 1173. Rory O'Connor made an agreement with Henry in 1175, called the **Treaty of Windsor.** Rory would remain High King of the non-Norman parts of Ireland, in return for a tribute from the kings under him. Despite this, Norman knights like John de Courcy continued to conquer Irish territory and O'Connor's authority collapsed. He was the last Irish High King.

## ACTIVITY

**Timeline**

Make a timeline of Henry II's involvement in Ireland. You should have entries for 1155, 1167, 1171, 1172 and 1175.

# UNIT 27: JOHN DE COURCY AND ULSTER

## WHO WAS JOHN DE COURCY?

We can learn quite a lot about the Normans in Ireland by studying a particular individual. We will look at the fortunes of a young Norman knight called **John de Courcy.** Many stories were told about John. He became a legend even in his own lifetime, so it is hard to tell fact from fiction.

In French, *de* means 'of' or 'from', and the de Courcy family came from Courcy in Normandy. John's ancestors had come to England with William the Conqueror in 1066. They were given land in Somerset in southern England. John was a younger son of the family and had no land of his own. He served King Henry II in his wars in France, and in 1176 he came to Dublin with William FitzAudelin, who was briefly the governor of Ireland.

War provided many young Norman knights with their only real chance of getting land and becoming rich. If they fought bravely and well, the king or someone else might reward them with land from the conquered territory. John had been unlucky so far. Henry II had not rewarded him.

An artist's impression of John de Courcy

## ACTIVITY

Find Somerset on a map of Britain. Explain to a partner why John de Courcy decided to leave his home in Somerset.

Here is a description of John de Courcy, written by Gerald of Wales:

> *John was fair haired and tall, with bony and sinewy limbs. His frame was lanky and he had a very strong physique, immense bodily strength and an extraordinarily bold temperament. He was a man of courage and a born fighter. In war he was impetuous. Away from the battlefield he was modest and restrained, and he gave the church of Christ that honour which is its due.*

## RESEARCH

As an historian, you want to know if Gerald's description of John de Courcy is likely to be true.

Write out the steps that you will need to take in order to ascertain this. What points will you have to consider?

Now find out!

Come to a conclusion and justify it to the class.

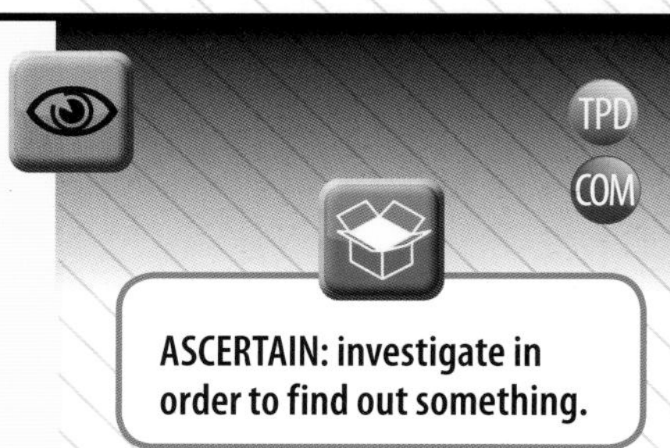

You remember that John de Courcy had come to Dublin in 1176 with the new governor of Ireland, William FitzAudelin. Here is what Gerald of Wales said John thought of FitzAudelin:

> ***Now John de Courcy saw that FitzAudelin was acting entirely from motives of greed, cowardice and double dealing, and that he was neither trusted by the Normans, nor feared by the Irish. He therefore won over to his side some of the Dublin garrison. They had not been paid for some time, and were discontented because of FitzAudelin's laziness in not filling the money chests with booty from the Irish. John's followers were few in number, but good, brave men, the pick of the army. So with 22 knights and about 300 others, this brave knight boldly made an assault on Ulaid...***

A life size model, in Carrickfergus Castle, of John de Courcy on horse back, attended by a page boy.

# THE ATTACK ON ULAID

The death of the King of Tyrone, the previous High King, in 1166 (Unit 24) had resulted in the smaller Ulster kingdoms fighting each other now that there was no strong king to control them. It would seem that MacDunlevy, the King of Ulaid (modern Antrim and Down) may have copied Dermot MacMurrough by inviting the Normans to come to Ulster and help him fight the other kings.

De Courcy planned not just to help MacDunlevy, but to replace him as ruler. To justify his attack, de Courcy gave two reasons:

1 He claimed that Henry II, probably at Windsor in 1175, had promised him Ulster "if he could conquer it by force".

2 De Courcy collected prophetic writings, especially ones that might be fulfilled by him. One of those was the following:

> ***A white knight, astride a white horse, bearing a device of birds on his shield will be the first to enter Ulaid and overrun it with hostile intent.***

He was white-haired, and had a white horse and a shield with three eagles. Some writers think that de Courcy might have made up some of the prophecies himself.

In 1177, John de Courcy marched 22 knights and about 300 foot soldiers to Ulaid and arrived at Downpatrick. MacDunlevy retreated in fright, but soon recruited a large army from his allies and returned to Downpatrick to give battle. According to one account, he brought priests and monks who stood on a hill to pray for de Courcy's defeat. De Courcy sent his troops to attack the praying monks, and then went on to win the battle!

# DE COURCY AS LORD OF ULSTER

Carrickfergus Castle, built by John de Courcy

Despite having so few soldiers, John de Courcy was able to defeat the local Irish. Probably some Irish were fighting on his side too, but the superior weapons and armour of the Normans helped them to win victories even when outnumbered. De Courcy took over most of Down and Antrim and built castles on its borders. He made Carrickfergus his headquarters, and there he built his strongest castle. Today it is very famous and you can read more about it in Unit 30.

Although King Henry allowed de Courcy to be called the lord of 'Ulster', the lordship only included the area of the modern counties of Down and Antrim, ie the area of the kingdom of Ulaid, not the whole area now called Ulster.

John de Courcy realised how important it was to be accepted as a ruler by the local Irish people. He used religion to do this.

At Downpatrick, the headquarters of MacDunlevy had been a fortified hill, now called The Hill of Down.

De Courcy built a castle there and rebuilt the cathedral on a nearby hill. He named the cathedral after St Patrick. In 1185 de Courcy claimed that the bodies of St Patrick, St Columba (Columbcille) and St Brigid had been discovered there. This made Downpatrick an important religious site.

De Courcy had coins struck with the head of St Patrick on one side and his own head on the other. Since only kings were meant to have their heads on coins, what did this suggest? One of these coins is now in Down Co Museum.

Down Cathedral painted in 1863 by Thomas Semple. De Courcy named this cathedral after St Patrick. De Courcy's cathedral was rebuilt as shown, in the 19th century.

# THE DOWNFALL OF DE COURCY

John de Courcy ruled as lord of Ulster for 27 years and in his day was one of the most powerful Normans in Ireland. But the King's son, Prince John, was jealous of de Courcy and feared his power. Prince John had been made 'Lord of Ireland' by his father, but de Courcy's coins did not acknowledge John's lordship.

In 1189 Henry II died and his elder son Richard became King Richard I (1189–99). Then, in 1199, Prince John became king. In 1204 King John ordered Hugh de Lacy, the ruler of Meath, to invade Ulster and drive de Courcy out. After a short war, de Courcy fled abroad and lived the rest of his life in relative poverty. De Lacy was then given the title 'Earl of Ulster'.

The story of John de Courcy showed that a Norman knight could win land and power very quickly, but that it was important not to make enemies and, above all, to keep the favour of the King. De Courcy started his life with nothing but a name and ended his life the same way.

## ACTIVITY

**Extended writing**

In your own words, write a short Wikipedia entry for John de Courcy. Include text, a timeline, images and links.

## ACTIVITY

### Class discussion

Talk about the following questions.

1. Although John de Courcy conquered Ulaid by force and then ruled the territory for 27 years, he did not keep these lands to pass on to his heirs. What do you think were the main reasons for this?
2. De Courcy used several methods to be accepted as ruler of Ulaid. What were they?
3. Gerald of Wales said that de Courcy felt that FitzAudelin was acting from motives of greed, cowardice and double dealing. In the end, was de Courcy himself any different?

# UNIT 28: WALES, SCOTLAND AND THE NORMANS

## WALES

Wales is a land of mountains and valleys, surrounded on three sides by the sea. The Welsh had their own language and were descended from the Celts who lived in Britain before the Anglo-Saxons came. The Welsh had fought the Anglo-Saxons long before the Normans arrived.

The Normans invaded Wales and were able to take over land in the south and the east along the English border. These areas were known as the **marches,** and the Normans who lived there were known as **marcher lords.** The Welsh adapted well to the Norman conquest. Welsh archers served in the Norman armies that came to Ireland in 1170.

The northern Welsh were less easily subdued. They copied the English weapons and castles, but when the English were weakened by civil or foreign war, they rebelled. The most famous Welsh leader was Llywelyn the Great (1173–1240) who dreamed of a united independent Wales.

However, in 1272 Edward I, a very strong English king, came to the throne. He conquered the rest of Wales and built 17 new stone castles – at Carmarthen, Harlech, Beaumaris and other places. They were the biggest and most impressive castles to be built in Britain. Edward's eldest son was declared Prince of Wales.

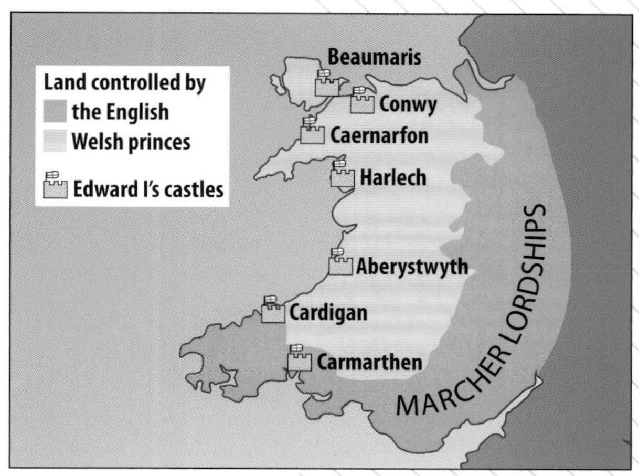

Harlech Castle, north Wales, built in 1283–89. The green area on the left was sea in 1283.

## ACTIVITY

Gerald of Wales, writing about 1194, described the Welsh like this:

> *Their only idea of tactics is either to follow their opponents or else run away from them. They cannot fight violently for very long or try to win a hand-to-hand fight. They may not do well in open fighting but they harass the enemy by ambushes and night attacks. In a single battle, they are easily beaten, but they are difficult to conquer in a long war, for they are not troubled by hunger or cold, fighting does not seem to tire them, they do not lose heart when things go wrong, and after one defeat they are ready to fight again and to face once more the hazards of war.*

1. According to Gerald's description, list the characteristics of the Welsh fighting methods, strengths and weaknesses.
2. Which do you think was the most significant strength in fighting the Normans?
3. Which do you think was the most significant weakness in fighting the Normans?
4. Do you think the Welsh were good fighters or bad fighters? Explain your opinion in about 100 words.

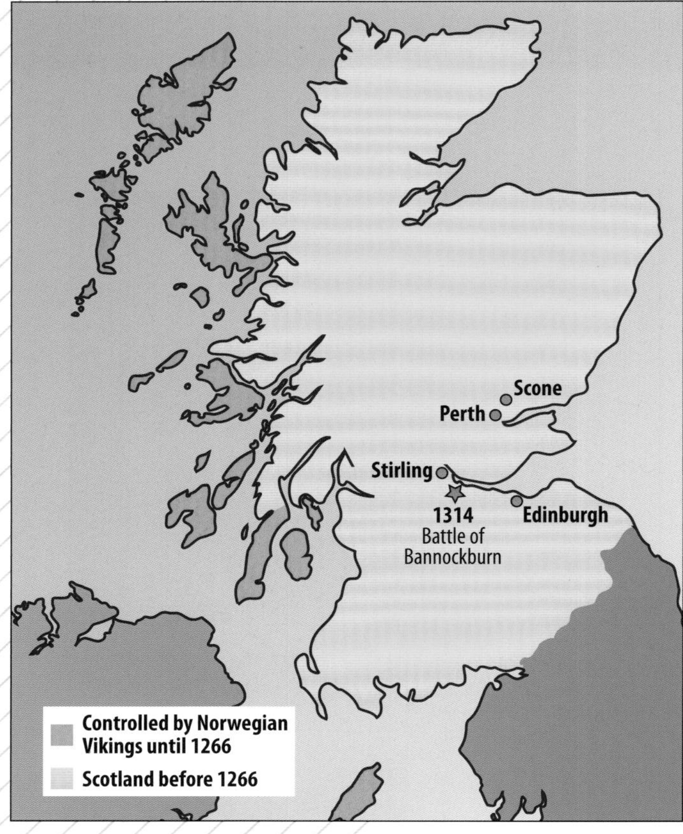


# SCOTLAND

Scotland was the last part of the British Isles to be invaded by the Normans and their successors. Scotland had its own kings and the Western Isles were ruled by Vikings from Norway. In the 12th century the Scots had even invaded the north of England. Sometimes the English kings tried to get the king of Scotland to submit to them so that they could control Scotland.

In the 13th century the Scottish kings became more powerful and took over the Viking areas. They were crowned at **Scone,** near Perth, on a special stone which was supposed to come from the Holy Land and to have been Jacob's pillow when he had the dream about the ladder reaching up to heaven (Genesis 28:11).

In 1286 the Scottish King Alexander III died with no heir, and the Scots asked King Edward I of England to pick a new king for them. This was a big mistake. It allowed Edward to meddle in Scotland. He invaded Scotland three times and stole the **Stone of Scone.** Up until 1996 it was kept in Westminster Abbey under the royal throne.

The Scots fought England fiercely, led first by **William Wallace** and then by **Robert the Bruce**. In 1314 Scottish independence was won when Robert the Bruce defeated Edward II at the **Battle of Bannockburn.** The Irish were so impressed by this victory that they invited Bruce to come to Ireland and help them fight the Normans. Robert's brother Edward arrived in 1316, but his success was short lived because he was killed in battle in 1318.

*In 1996 the British Government decided that the Stone of Scone should be given back to Scotland when not in use at coronations. On 15 November 1996, there was a handover ceremony at the Scottish border. The Stone was taken to Edinburgh Castle where it is now kept. If there is a coronation of a new king or queen in London, the Stone will be lent back for the occasion.*

This statue of Robert the Bruce is at Bannockburn in Scotland.

# UNIT 29: MOTTE AND BAILEY CASTLES

## THE EARLIEST CASTLES

If the Normans depended on their mounted knights and their armour to *win* control of England, Ireland and Wales, they depended on their castles to *keep* control of them. The earliest castles had to be built quickly. It could take ten years to build a stone castle, so the earliest castles were wooden. These wooden castles are called **motte and bailey** castles. The people the Normans had just conquered were usually forced to build the castles.

Here is how the Anglo-Saxon Chronicle put it in its entry for 1067:

> *He [William I] caused castles to be built which were a sore burden to the poor.*

Here is an entry for 1068:

> *When the King was informed that the people of the north had gathered together and would oppose him if he came, he marched to Nottingham and built a castle there, and so on to York, and there built two castles, and also in Lincoln, and in many other places in that part of the country.*

## ACTIVITY

ICT

Carry out the following task in pairs. *The York Daily News* of February 1068 is running a story on the advance of William and the effects of his castle-building on the people of the town. You are sent out to interview people in the street to gather their views. Take turns with your partner in being the reporter and the interviewee.

You interview:

- A young peasant Anglo-Saxon who is just getting his piece of land ready for sowing in the spring. His wife is expecting their first baby in April.
- A widow who has heard of the Normans and is interested to know about Norman fashion.
- A leather worker who makes saddles and bridles, gloves and shoes.
- Think of one other person you could interview.

When you have gathered all your facts and opinions, write an article for the newspaper. Remember to have a good headline.

What photographs would suit your article?

# PARTS OF THE CASTLE

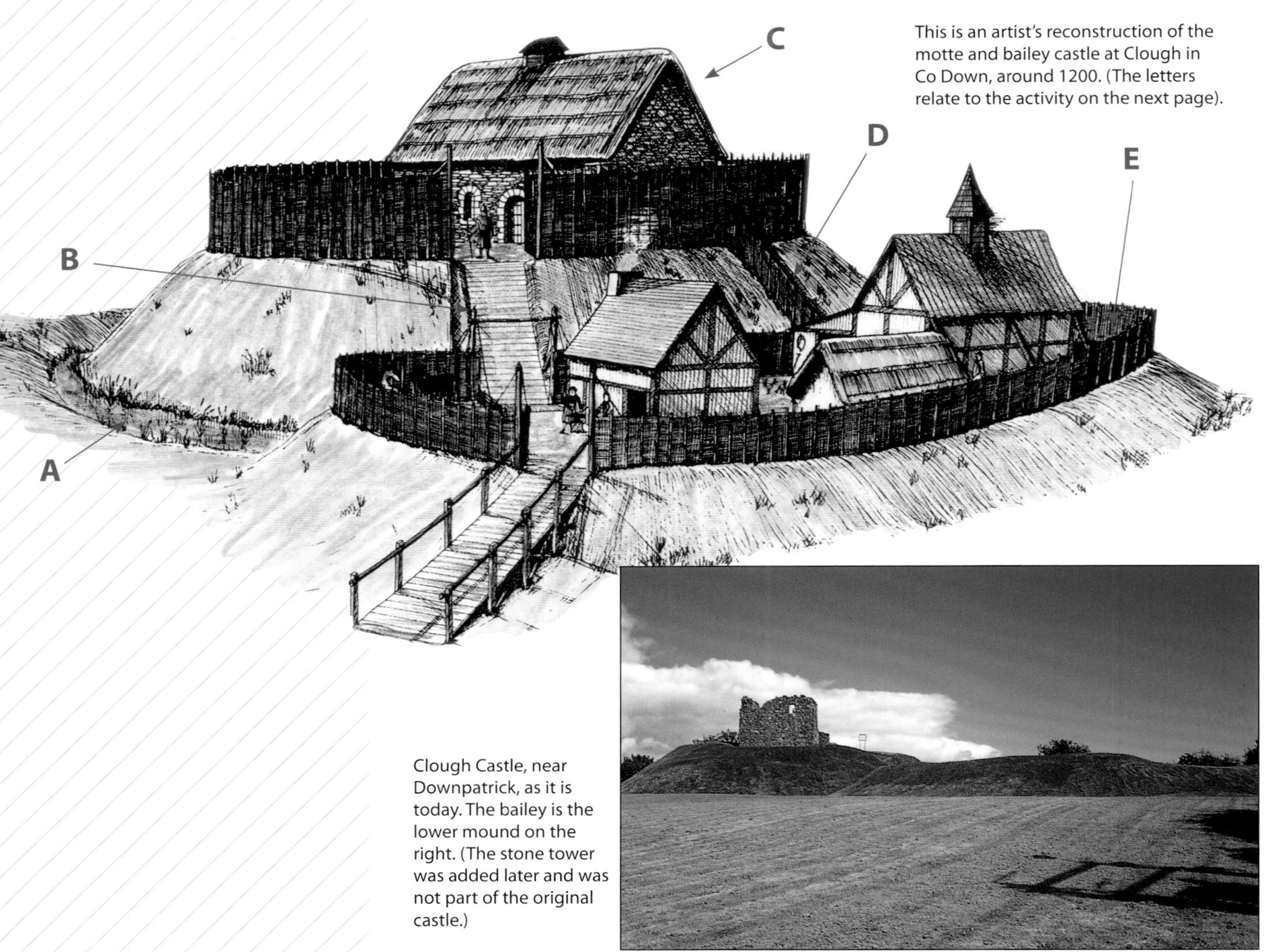


This is an artist's reconstruction of the motte and bailey castle at Clough in Co Down, around 1200. (The letters relate to the activity on the next page).

Clough Castle, near Downpatrick, as it is today. The bailey is the lower mound on the right. (The stone tower was added later and was not part of the original castle.)

The main parts of a motte and bailey castle were:

- **The motte:** this was a small hill or earthwork made by digging a large circular ditch and throwing the soil up in the centre.
- **The keep:** This was a tower built on top of the motte as a lookout. Occasionally, as at Clough, the wooden keep might later be replaced by a stone keep.
- **The bailey:** This was an enclosed area, usually on a smaller earthwork than the motte. Here the soldiers lived and slept.
- **The moat:** This is the name given to the deep ditch surrounding the whole castle. Occasionally, but not often, it was filled with water.
- **Wooden bridge:** This connected the keep to the bailey. Defenders smashed it if they had to retreat to the keep.

## ACTIVITY

Look at the artist's reconstruction of Clough Castle.
Identify the parts of the castle marked A–E.

## ACTIVITY

Divide the class into attackers and defenders of Clough Castle. One group plans the defence of the castle and the other the attack. What are the weaknesses and strengths of motte and bailey castles? Who do you think will win?

A Norman knight has just ridden into the castle (from an original painting at the former Ulster History Park, near Omagh).

## ACTIVITY

Talk about this picture in class.

Describe everything that you see in it.

What part of the castle do you think this is?

What do you feel is the mood of the picture?

Now imagine you are the young man holding the shield. Write a diary entry telling of the events leading up to the moment shown in the picture.

# UNIT 30: STONE CASTLES

CRUSADES: a series of campaigns, between 1095 and 1291, fought by European countries in order to regain control of the Holy Land from Muslim rule.

MACHICOLATIONS: holes in the walls of a castle to let objects or boiling oil be dropped on attackers below.

## KEEP-IN-BAILEY CASTLES

As soon as they could, the Normans began to replace their motte and bailey castles with stone castles. Early castles were still built on mottes, and square cornered towers were common. Later the Crusaders went to the Holy Land and copied the new castle building techniques that they saw there. Round towers and castles with curtain walls and machicolations became more common.

The commonest type of castle was the **keep-in-bailey castle.** This had a stone keep surrounded by a curtain wall. Sometimes the keep formed part of the outer wall. Keep-in-bailey castles were built mostly in the 12th and 13th centuries.

### CARRICKFERGUS CASTLE

1195

1222

We have already mentioned Carrickfergus Castle, which was first built by John de Courcy. It is an example of a keep-in-bailey castle. The picture above shows how the castle looked once it was completed around 1195.

After Hugh de Lacy had replaced John de Courcy, King John of England controlled the castle himself for a time. He ordered some improvements to be made. The picture on the left is how the castle looked around 1222, once these changes had been made.

Compare the first two pictures. What changes have been made? Why do you think King John might have made these changes? Why do you think John de Courcy chose this site for his castle in the first place?

Later still, Hugh de Lacy was given back control of the castle. He made even more changes. This is how the castle looked around 1242 after he had finished his work (note that it is viewed from a slightly different angle).

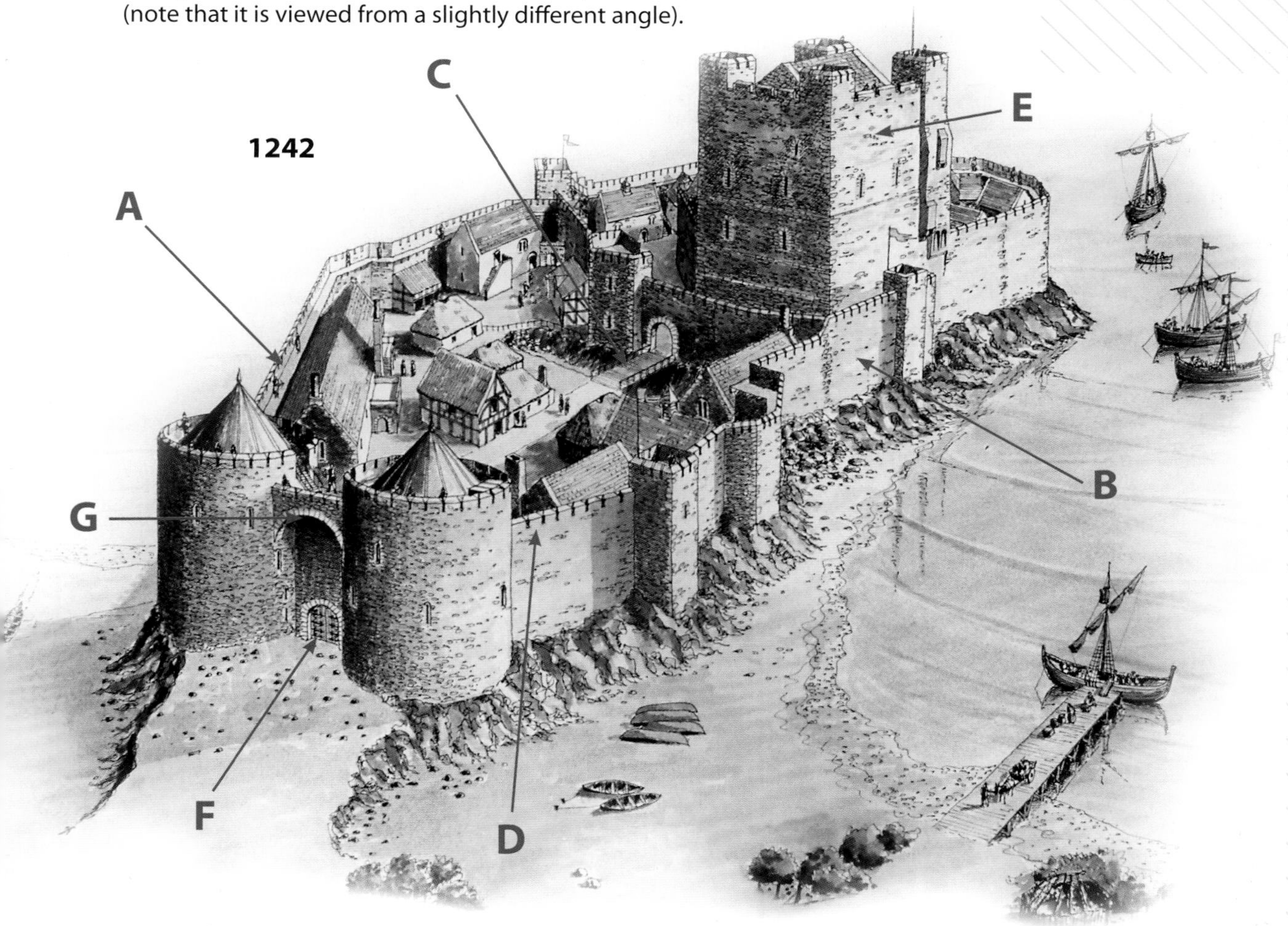

**1242**

What changes have been made this time? Do you think these changes would make the castle safer? Would it be easier or more difficult to capture? Explain your answer.

The important parts of the castle are marked with letters on the picture above. These are:

- A – Wall walk
- B – Curtain wall
- C – Drawbridge (over ditch beside interior wall)
- D – Merlons (small walls) with embrasures (spaces) between for shooting arrows.
- E – Keep
- F – Gatehouse with two towers and portcullis
- G – Machicolation

Sometimes (most often in England and Wales) a castle was built with two concentric curtain walls. The space between the two walls was called the **outer bailey**, while the keep was built inside the inner wall in the **inner bailey**. This is called a **concentric castle**. An example is Beaumaris Castle in Wales. These were usually built in the 14th century.

# TOWER HOUSES

The drawing is of Jordan's Castle in Ardglass, Co Down. This is a **tower house** and is the commonest type of castle in Ireland. A tower house has no curtain wall at all and consists only of a keep. Most have four floors. They were built mostly in the 15th century.

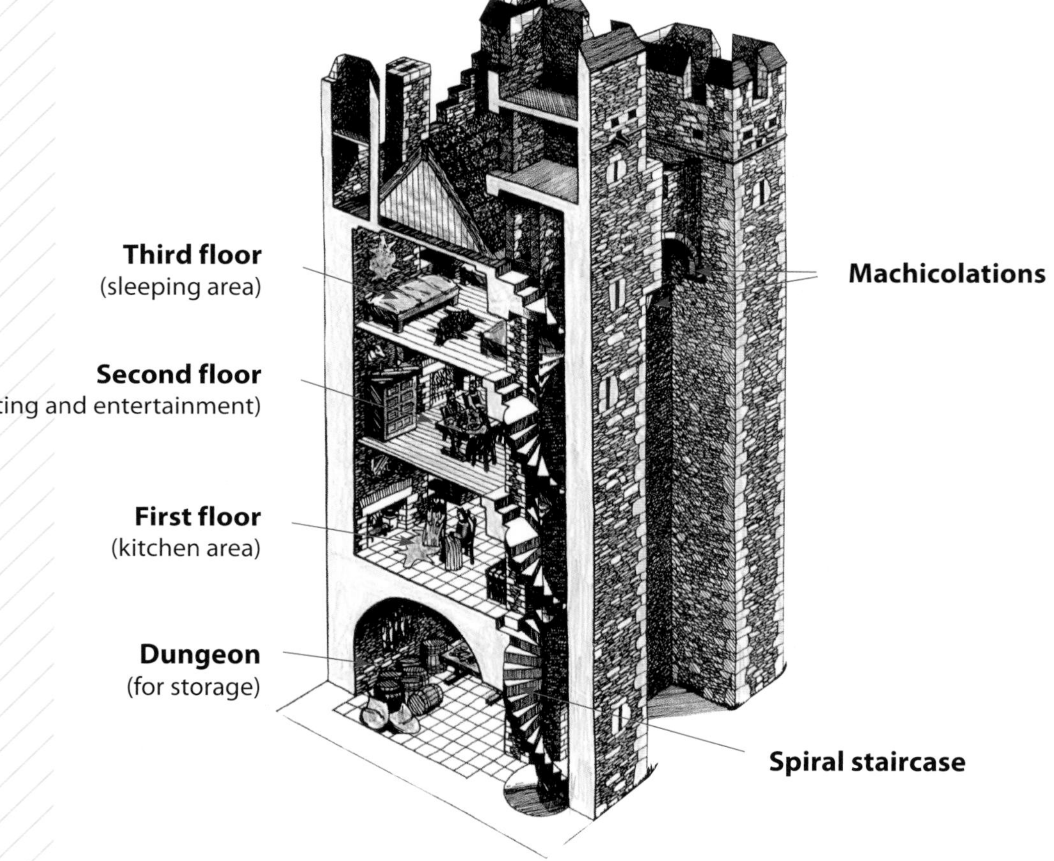

## ACTIVITY

What do you think it would be like to live in a tower house like this if you were:

- The owner of the tower house
- The Lady of the house
- A soldier who kept watch on the battlements
- A stable boy

# UNIT 31: MEDIEVAL WARFARE

## KNIGHTS

In the Middle Ages, knights had to be available for 40 days of military service every year. A fully armed knight needed a lance, shield, sword, horse and full armour.

In Norman times the basic armour was a **hauberk (**long coat) of chain mail (see Unit 18), and a metal **helmet.** As time went on, armour became more complex. Plate armour replaced mail, and every part of the body was covered. A full suit could weigh 27 kilogrammes. If a knight in full armour fell over, it took a lot of strength to get up again.

Some knights fought with a **mace** which was a hand held weapon about 50 cms long, with a heavy metal ball at one end, often with spikes. It was used to smash an opponent's skull or his arm.

## ACTIVITY

SM

How good a Norman soldier would you be? Put together something that weighs 27 kilos, for example bags of sugar or flour, in a bin bag.
How far can you walk with it?

As well as fighting for their king, knights also took part in **jousting** competitions to show off their skill and courage. This involved two knights on horseback riding towards each other and attempting to knock their opponent off their horse with a long pole called a lance. Even though it was a sport, it was quite dangerous and many knights were wounded or even killed while jousting.

Froissart was an historian of the 14th century. Here is his description of a good joust:

> *The two knights spurred forward and met this time with straight lances, hitting each other clean and hard on their shields. Both were nearly knocked to the ground, but they gripped their horses with their legs and stayed on... This joust was very highly applauded and both French and English said (they) had jousted admirably, without either sparing themselves or causing each other an injury.*

Medieval jousting being staged at Littlecote Manor, Berkshire. The knights carry a traditional lance (used to impale opponents) but deliberately blunted for jousting.

SIEGE: To surround and attack a castle.

# SIEGE WARFARE

A **trebuchet** was a large siege 'engine' used to fling heavy stones against castle walls. It worked like a large see-saw. Weights, or people pulling on ropes, brought one side down suddenly and the other side had a sling that flung the stone.

A **catapult** was like the trebuchet. It fired a heavy stone, but it worked by tension ropes, instead of counterweights.

A **siege tower** was used to reach the top of a castle or town wall. Soldiers crossed from the top of the tower onto the wall using a ramp. It was used in Europe and in the Crusades but not in the British Isles.

A trebuchet

A siege tower

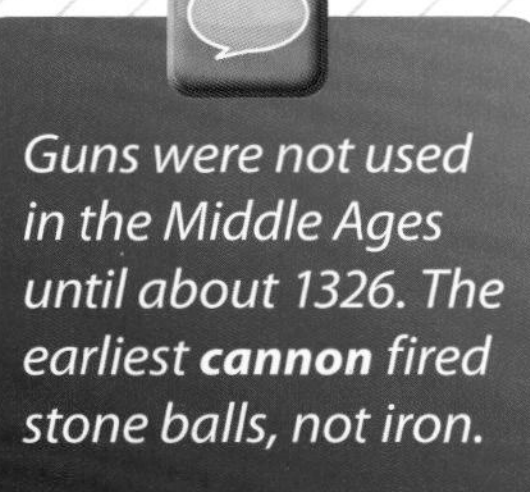

*Guns were not used in the Middle Ages until about 1326. The earliest **cannon** fired stone balls, not iron.*

A **battering ram** was a very large piece of wood that soldiers could use to break down the door of a castle. Often it had wheels and a roof to protect the soldiers from arrows.

Think about the four devices used in siege warfare. How effective do you think each would be as a way of attacking a stone castle? What would be the advantages and dangers of these devices for the attackers?

## PROJECT

In groups of three or four, use matchboxes, lollipop sticks, plasticine or any other suitable materials, to make a model of a siege tower or a trebuchet.

# BOWS

The **short bow** was used by the Normans in 1066 and on into the 12th century. The bow was about 1.2 metres long and had a range of 250 metres.

The commonest bow in the later Middle Ages was the **longbow.** It was about two metres long and had a range of 300 metres. You had to be very strong to use it, so early training was necessary.

RANGE: The furthest distance that the arrow could go.

Here is what Froissart wrote about this around 1370:

> *Again in this year it was advised and decreed that throughout the realms of England, no man should use any play or pastime save only the longbow and arrows, on pain of death, and that every bow-maker and arrow-maker should have his debts cancelled.*

The **crossbow** was held horizontally and shot bolts (heavy short arrows). The string had to be wound back and could fire with a high speed. It was useful for defending a castle because it was very accurate, but it took twelve times as long to reload as a longbow.

A model of a crossbow man at Carrickfergus Castle.

Full size model of an archer on the battlements of Carrickfergus Castle.

A model of a 14th century 'man at arms', guarding the entrance to Carrickfergus Castle.

A group of historians wants to create life-size models, like those in the photographs, to place in a restored 13th century castle. How do they get their information to make sure that the models are accurate?

# UNIT 32: LIFE IN A CASTLE

## ROOMS

What was it like to live in a castle? Today it is possible to visit many real castles and get some idea of what they were like. Three castles that have furniture and are well worth visiting are:

- Carrickfergus Castle, Co Antrim
- Jordan's Castle, Ardglass, Co Down
- Bunratty Castle, Co Clare

We will look at some pictures from **Carrickfergus Castle.** Since castles were really defensive buildings, they were not very comfortable to live in. They were cold, damp and draughty. Today the windows usually have glass in them, but in the Middle Ages castle windows had only shutters. The keep of a castle usually contained the living quarters, and Jordan's Castle in Unit 30 is fairly typical.

Left: The great hall set for banquet. The lord sat on the raised platform at the end of the room. Walls were decorated with tapestries. Long trestle tables were set up specially for the meal. The great hall was the most important room in the castle. It had a tall ceiling and was used for banquets and entertainment like dances. The lord held court (met people) here too. Sometimes there was a small gallery for musicians. During the day everyone ate in the great hall, and at night most of the soldiers and servants slept here on straw.

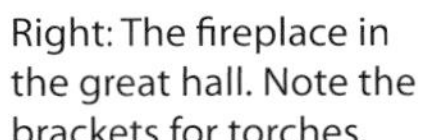

Right: The fireplace in the great hall. Note the brackets for torches.

Left: King John on the 'John'! Toilets in medieval times were usually in the corners of towers. A hole ran through the stonework to the outer wall. Sometimes clothes were hung over toilets because people thought that the smell kept away moths. This is why the toilet was called the 'garderobe'.

Right: Castles usually needed a steward to look after the day to day running. Here the steward of Carrickfergus Castle is seen doing his accounts with a quill pen.

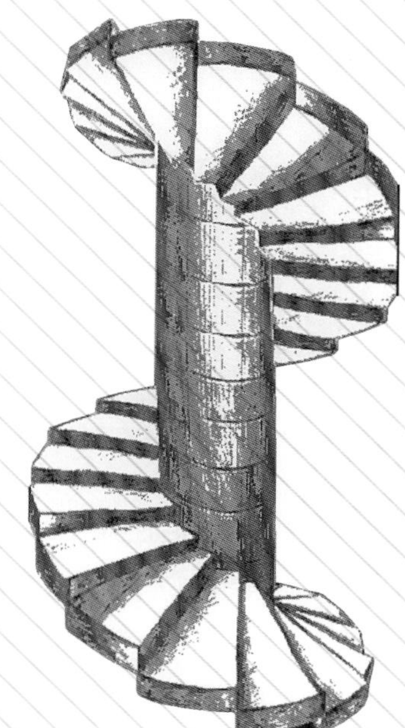

To save space, staircases were spiral and built into a corner. Going up, they went clockwise.

How did this help a defender? (Clue: swords were usually carried in the right hand.)

You have learnt that the great hall was the most important room in the castle. Everybody gathered there and many even slept there, with a central brazier for heat. By the end of the 13th century, the lord's family were beginning to look for more privacy for themselves and smaller rooms just for them began to be constructed. Here is what one poet, William Langland, wrote about this trend:

*"Woe is in the hall each day in the week.*
*There the lord and lady like not to sit.*
*Now every rich man eats by himself*
*In a private parlor to be rid of poor men,*
*Or in a chamber with a chimney*
*And leaves the great hall."*

Can you see any connection between the evolution of the great hall and the design of houses today?

## FOOD

Here is some typical food eaten in a castle:

**Breakfast**: bread soaked in ale or watered wine.

**Main meal (11.00 am)**: Mostly meat – usually beef and mutton, but sometimes venison and poultry.

**Common vegetables**: dried peas and beans, onions, garlic, herbs.

**Banquets**: Meat was often served from the table and eaten with hands. Forks were almost unknown. Manners were terrible. You could throw used bones on the floor and it was okay to burp!

## ACTIVITY

How healthy do you believe this diet would be?

What would a normal family eat today?

Design a 14th century menu and a comparative healthy 21st century menu.

# WOMEN

The lord's wife, daughters and relatives were very important in the castle. They usually had their own private rooms. Since the entrances to most rooms had curtains and no doors, beds were fitted with curtains. You undressed by kneeling on the bed with the curtains drawn around you.

Most women in a castle had to spin and weave cloth. If the lord was away, his lady was responsible for running the castle. High ranking women had their own 'ladies in waiting' (servants).

## ACTIVITY

Here is an extract from the will of Edward the Black Prince in 1376.

> *We give to [Canterbury Cathedral]... our chamber hangings of black tapestry with a red border and swans with the heads of ladies... The blue clothing with golden roses and ostrich feathers we give to our son Richard, together with the bed that we have of the same suite and all the apparel [bedclothes] of the said bed which our father the King gave us...*

1. What impression does this give you of the possessions of a lord at this time?
2. In castles, tapestries were often hung on the walls. What are the equivalents of tapestries today?
3. Draw your own version of what the tapestries described may have looked like.

1. Describe a typical day in a medieval castle.
2. In what ways is life in a castle different to life in your house? List as many ways as you can.
3. Are there any things that have remained the same, or nearly the same?
4. What kinds of things do people have to manage no matter when they lived?

## PROJECT

Design your own castle. You can choose either a motte and bailey castle or a stone castle. Draw or paint your design and explain what each part of your castle is for. Perhaps you could put up your designs in the classroom, or have a go at building a model of your castle at home.

# UNIT 33: THE MEDIEVAL VILLAGE

## THE VILLAGE OF THE MANOR

In the Middle Ages most people lived in a village. There might be 20 to 30 families living in a village, as well as a knight or lord. The most important buildings in the village were the church, the manor house (a fortified house or small castle where the lord lived) and the mill. The lord controlled everything that happened in the village and the peasant villagers had to do what he said. For example they had to:

- work several days a week on his farmland;
- marry the person he told them to;
- use only fallen wood for their fires.

Two peasants ploughing, shown on the Bayeux Tapestry.

## ACTIVITY

BC

Study the picture of ploughing from the Bayeux Tapestry.
What might these two men be saying to each other? In pairs, make up a funny conversation that they might be having. Perform the exchanges in class and vote on the one you think is the funniest!

## FARMING

The land belonging to a village was strictly controlled. The land used for growing crops was usually divided into two or three huge fields (often up to 200 acres, roughly one square kilometre). These huge fields were called **open fields** as no fences or hedges ran across them. Other land was used to grow hay for the winter, and there was uncultivated **common land** where everyone had the right to graze animals.

On the edges of the village was the forest. Here pigs could be grazed and firewood could be collected – but **not** cut – from trees. Peasants could also gather nuts, berries, herbs and wild honey.

Why do you think peasants could collect only fallen wood and not cut wood from trees?

The large open fields were divided into long narrow **strips** and each peasant could have two, three or four strips in each field. The strips were not always side by side and a lot of time was wasted going from one strip to another. Between each strip was a ditch and this wasted valuable land. Everyone had to grow the same crop in each field, so the system discouraged peasants from trying something different.

## ACTIVITY

About 1390, William Langland wrote a poem called 'Piers Plowman'. Here is an adaptation of his description of a ploughman:

> *His coat was of coarse material, his hood was full of holes and his hair stuck out of it. As he trod the soil his toes stuck out of his worn shoes with their thick soles; his stockings hung about his shins on all sides and he was covered with mud as he followed the plough. He had two mittens scantily made of rough stuff, with worn out fingers and thick with muck.*

Discuss the value of this extract as an historical source. Think about:

- whether it is a primary or secondary source
- whether it is biased or neutral

What else would you need to know in order to evaluate this extract fully?

Draw a picture of this ploughman.

Life was very hard for peasant women too. Here are some duties of a good wife as set out in 1393:

> *Let her go often into the fields to see how they are working... and let her make them get up in the morning. If she be a good housewife, let her rise by herself... go to the window and shout until she sees them come running out, for they are given to laziness.*

This a plan of a typical medieval village. Can you see the East, West and South fields?

## CROP ROTATION

Crops were **rotated** round the fields so that the same crops were not grown in the same field for two years in a row. Every third year the land was left fallow, to help the soil recover. This is known as **three-field crop rotation.** Here is an example of how the people in this village may have planned their cultivation:

| | West Field | South Field | East Field |
|---|---|---|---|
| 1251 | Wheat | Barley or Oats | Fallow |
| 1252 | Barley or Oats | Fallow | Wheat |
| 1253 | Fallow | Wheat | Barley or Oats |
| 1254 | Wheat | Barley or Oats | Fallow |
| 1255 | Barley or Oats | Fallow | Wheat |

**FALLOW:** land left ploughed over; but nothing cultivated in it and weeds allowed to grow.

## RESEARCH

Divide the class into groups of three or four.

Find out about crop rotation. Is it still practised today?

If possible, interview a farmer for this task. Put together a questionnaire to bring with you when you meet the farmer.

In your group, discuss what information you need to get and what questions you will need to ask to get this information.

Ask questions such as:

- What crops does the farmer grow?
- What are the reasons for crop rotation?
- What might happen if it was not done?

You may think of more questions yourselves.

Put your findings together neatly in a word processed document. Remember to include as many details as you can. Perhaps you might be able to take photographs to illustrate your report.

Sowing and harrowing portrayed on the Bayeux Tapestry.

In farming, what is 'harrowing'?

## BY-LAWS

Villages could have their own laws, called by-laws, that applied only to that village. Here are some village by-laws of 1293:

1 *No one shall enter the fields with a cart to carry grain after sunset.*
2 *No one shall enter the fields except at the village entrances.*
3 *All grain collected in the fields shall be taken out openly through the middle of the town and not secretly by back ways.*

Can you explain the reasons for these rules? (Tip: All grain was harvested together and divided according to the number of strips each peasant had.)

WO

## ACTIVITY

Form into groups and create a list of by-laws for either (i) your classroom, or (ii) your school, or (iii) your home.

# HOUSES

This is a reconstruction of a timber-framed house in the former Ulster History Park near Omagh, Co Tyrone. Medieval house construction was a bit like this.

Most ordinary peasants lived in small one-roomed houses. The frame of the house was wooden and the walls were made of **wattle and daub.** A wattle wall or fence was made of wood or branches woven together. It could then be plastered over with mud mixture called daub.

Often there were no windows, only a door. Cooking was done in a pot over an open fire in the middle of the room, and smoke escaped through a hole in the thatched roof. In areas where there was no timber, houses were made of stone.

People lived in one half of the house, and at night animals such as pigs and oxen slept in the other end. There wasn't much furniture – a few three-legged stools, a bench table, and maybe a chest for clothes. The bed was little more than a mattress stuffed with straw.

## ACTIVITY

Close the classroom curtains and make the room as dark as you can.

Be very quiet! Imagine that you belong to a peasant family in the 13th century. It is the middle of the night, you are lying on your straw mattress, and you have woken up.

What do you feel?
What do you think?
What do you smell?
What do you hear?
What can you see?

Whisper your ideas softly as you think of them.

This is a drawing of what a peasant's house would have looked like.

## ACTIVITY

### Class discussion

If you were told you were going to be turned into a peasant in 1250, would you rather be a man or a woman? Explain your choice.

# UNIT 34: THE MEDIEVAL TOWN

## THE BEGINNING OF TOWNS

Towns became very important in the Middle Ages. Most towns were small compared to our towns today. Only 10,000 people lived in London in Norman times and York had about 5,000.

Towns started for many different reasons. In Ireland the earliest towns were ports. Others, like Downpatrick and Armagh, grew up around religious centres. Some, like Carrickfergus and Trim, grew up around an important castle. In our study of the medieval town we will look at Irish examples – Carlingford in Co Louth and Tralee in Co Kerry. In Tralee the atmosphere of a medieval town has been recreated by a special exhibition called *Geraldine Tralee,* in Kerry County Museum. Here you can travel back in time and experience not only the sights, but also the sounds and smells of a medieval town. You can see some pictures taken at *Geraldine Tralee* in this unit.

The leatherworker from Geraldine Tralee. Notice how poor medieval people did not wear very colourful clothing.

A street in Carlingford, Co Louth. This was a Norman settlement. Carlingford still has many features of a medieval town, such as narrow streets. The tower house in the background is believed to have been a mint.

**MINT: a place where coins are made.**

Often a lord of the manor encouraged the development of a town. Tralee was founded by John FitzThomas FitzGerald in 1216. He also established a Dominican monastery there.

Lords liked towns because there were more people to pay taxes and if the town had a market, everyone selling goods had to pay a tax to the lord. However, as towns developed the townspeople began to resent paying taxes to the lord and often bought their freedom.

When a lord gave up control of a town the citizens were granted a **charter**. Often these were bought from the king. When a town got its charter it became a **borough** and each citizen who owned a house or business was called a **burgess.** Burgesses could elect a mayor and town council to run the town. They paved the streets, organised a night watch and made regulations about the town. A town with a charter still often had to pay rent to the lord who owned the land it was on, but they didn't have to pay taxes on trade in the town any more.

Here is an example of a Charter:

*A Charter*

*By the grace of God, Henry, King of England, greets you the people of Someton. Know ye that I have granted to the people of Someton all those customs that they enjoyed in the time of my grandfather.*

1 *The right of toll. [This allowed the people to charge traders entering the town.]*
2 *The right to hold a market on Tuesdays.*
3 *The right of theam. [This allowed the town to control the courts and keep any fines paid.]*
4 *Freedom for any man who lives in the town for a year and a day without being claimed by his overlord.*

*Signed this 3rd of October, 1161*
*Henry II*

## ACTIVITY

On an outline map of Ireland, mark the following towns:

| | | | |
|---|---|---|---|
| **Tralee** | **Carlingford** | **Carrickfergus** | **Downpatrick** |
| **Armagh** | **Dublin** | **Waterford** | **Cork** |

Medieval towns were usually walled. This is a gate on the walls around Carlingford. Traders entering through gates to sell in the town had to pay a toll. The building above this gate was the jail.

# THE TOWN WALLS

Most medieval towns were walled, and there were good reasons for this. Towns were rich and were a temptation to thieves. A wall made the town secure at night, and could keep out other undesirables like people with diseases. Town walls were not really designed for defence although a large city might run the risk of attack. A wall was often added when the town was well established and was a status symbol. The townspeople were really saying *"We* are important, because we have a wall round *our* town."

The walls were usually plain curtain walls with modest gateways like the one in the photograph, at Carlingford. Entry to the town was strictly controlled and traders were charged a toll (a payment). At night the gates were closed and no one was allowed in or out. The town was patrolled by the night watch who kept a lookout for thieves and outbreaks of fire.

Why do you think the night watch had to look out for fires?

# LIFE IN A TOWN

What were medieval towns really like?

They were very small by our standards. Tralee was granted a charter in 1286 and a document from 1298 records that the businesses were paying 100 shillings in annual rent to the Fitzgeralds (Geraldines) who owned the town. This rent suggests that Tralee had a population of 500 to 600 people.

Towns were noisy and smelly. Most people threw their rubbish out into the street and emptied their chamber pots (used before flushable toilets were invented) straight out of the bedroom window. A narrow drain along the edge of the street carried this away – but only when it rained! Areas near butchers were particularly smelly because they threw out offal and rotten meat. The town council often made all the butchers live in one street to keep the problem all in one place. There are still towns today with a street called 'The Shambles'. This word means a street where the butchers are. One of the most famous is in York.

The streets were very narrow. Many of the buildings were timber framed with each floor wider than the one below. If you leaned out far enough through a very high window you could shake hands with your neighbour across the street! You can see this in the picture of The Shambles in York on the right.

Craftsmen and traders usually made the things they sold in small workshops in their own houses. Living above their shop made it easy to keep an eye on things. Women often played an active part in the family business or might even run their own. Most people just made or sold one thing, like shoes, hats, bread, or pies.

Once a wall was built the town could not get any bigger. Sometimes only the Anglo-Normans were allowed to live in the town, and the native Irish built houses outside the walls. These settlements were sometimes called **Irishtown**.

The Shambles, York – a street of butchers. This is one of the best preserved medieval streets in England. Notice how each floor juts out over the floor below.

**OFFAL: bits of butchered animals that aren't eaten – like the guts.**

The butcher's stall from Geraldine Tralee. Can you identify the different things the butcher is selling? The woman's headdress is called a wimple.

## ACTIVITY

Here is a photograph of the blacksmith's forge, Geraldine Tralee. Study this picture and answer the questions that follow.

1. Why do you think the boy is watching the blacksmith?
2. What is the person in the background doing?
3. What might the blacksmith have bought from the leatherworker (page 105)?
4. Why has the blacksmith put straw on the floor?
5. What would be the sights, sounds and smells of this forge?

# LAW AND ORDER

Some traders were dishonest. Traders used scales to weigh goods to work out how much they were worth, but some people kept two sets of scales – one for buying and the other for selling! Guess which one over-weighed the goods? Others used dangerous ingredients like arsenic, or added chalk dust instead of flour to bread. Anyone caught cheating was put in the stocks (holding your feet) or the pillory (head and hands) for a day. People then could pelt them with mud, or eggs or empty a chamber pot over them!

WO

## ACTIVITY

**Class debate**

Organise a class debate on the following motion:
"This house believes that the pillory and stocks were a good idea and should be brought back as a punishment."

# CRAFTSMEN AND APPRENTICES

Many different trades could be found in a town. These included carpenters, coopers, drapers, embroiderers, glovers, hosiers, furriers, potters, shoemakers, smiths, tailors, and weavers. Different kinds of food were sold by bakers, grocers, vintners, butchers, fishmongers, poulterers etc. There were also general merchants who imported unusual goods from England, Europe and even further afield. Merchants often became very rich but the risks were high because of piracy at sea and robbers on land.

**UTENSILS: tools or containers, usually domestic, like cups and forks.**

## ACTIVITY

Write down all the trades listed in the paragraph above. Beside each one, write a description of what they did.

Which of these names have become surnames?

Can you think of any other jobs which have become surnames? For example 'Turner' comes from the trade of turning wood on a wheel to make utensils.

In many towns, **guilds** controlled all trades. You could only practice a trade if the guild allowed you to. The guilds controlled the prices that people charged and the quality of the goods. To enter a trade you had to become an **apprentice** to a master (at a young age, perhaps even at the age of seven) and serve your time for seven years. Once qualified you became a **journeyman** which allowed you to get a wage of several pence a day (the French word for a working day is journée). If a journeyman wanted to become independent he had to become a **master craftsman,** but only if the guild allowed. To qualify he had to do a test piece of work, called a **masterpiece.** If he was good enough and if there were not enough in that particular trade, he then became a master.

## ACTIVITY

Look at the pictures in this Unit and write a description of how medieval townspeople dressed. Write a paragraph each on women, men and boys.

## ACTIVITY

Create a mind map, showing the differences between living in a town today and in medieval times. You might start like this:

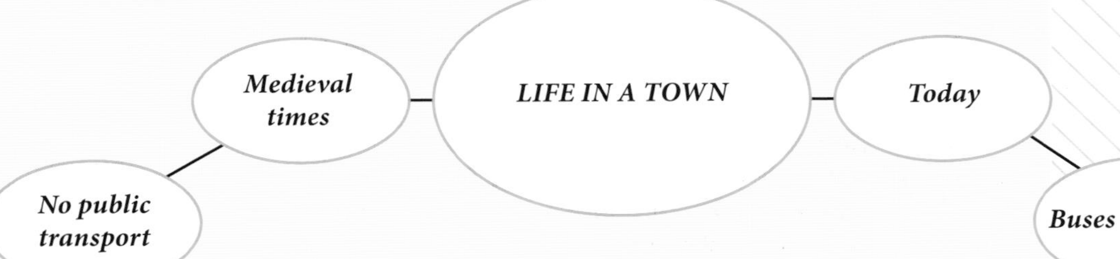

THE HIGH MIDDLE AGES

# UNIT 35: THE CHURCH

## THE POWER OF THE CHURCH

The magnificent west front of the Early English style cathedral at Salisbury in England. Note the tall narrow windows, the lead roof, and the flying buttresses to support the walls.

In the Middle Ages everyone in western and central Europe was Roman Catholic, except for some Jews. Everyone had to attend church and the church was very powerful. The head of the whole church in Europe was the **Pope** in Rome. He was more powerful than any king and even emperors were supposed to obey him.

The church was very important for ordinary people. There was a church in every village, and it was the centre of their lives. Although the services were in Latin, tapestries, wall hangings and stained glass windows showed vivid images of Heaven, Hell and the demons. To most people, Hell was as real as their own house, and no one wanted to go there.

Here is how one medieval monk described Hell:

> *There were trees on fire, and sinners being tortured on those trees. Some were hung by their feet, some by their hair, and some by the arm. There was a furnace burning with seven flames, and many sinners were punished in it. It had a fiery wheel which was turned a thousand times every day by an evil angel. At each turn a thousand sinners were burnt on it.*

The church was very wealthy because it owned a quarter of all the land in England. Wealthy nobles and kings often left land to the church so that their souls could be prayed for. The bishops and archbishops were chosen by the Pope and were usually from noble families. Because churchmen understood Latin and were educated, they usually helped the king to rule the country.

## THE CHURCH AND THE PEOPLE

**ALMS: money given to the poor.**

Most people loved the church. Life was full of hardships like famine, disease and poverty. The church brought comfort by offering poor people hope for the future. If you obeyed the priests and did not annoy God, you would go to Heaven to be with Christ and his angels. And if you were sick, God might heal you.

The church offered practical help too. They had to look after the poor by giving out **alms**. They ran the only hospitals and because priests and monks were educated, they ran the only schools.

The church regulated holidays (Holy days) and put on special events like processions and mystery plays. They taught people to obey the king and to respect their lords. Most people believed in real miracles and believed that holy relics held the power to heal them.

Gerald of Wales wrote down this story of a miracle in the 12th century:

> *A boy tried to steal some young pigeons from a nest in Saint David's church. His hand stuck to the stone on which he was leaning. No doubt this was punishment from the Saint, who was protecting the birds in his own church. For three days and nights the boy, with his parents and friends, prayed at the church alter. On the third day, by God's action, the power which held his hand loosened. He was freed from the force which bound him to the stone. The stone is preserved to this day. The marks of the boy's fingers where he pressed on the stone can be clearly seen, as if it were wax.*

Do you think Gerald believes this story? Give reasons for your opinion.

## CHURCH ARCHITECTURE

The Normans introduced bigger and better churches than had ever been seen before. Until about 1180 churches had windows and doors with rounded arches. Then the **Gothic** style appeared from France, with much thinner walls and pointed arches.

Gothic architecture came in three main phases:

**1 Early English:** about 1180–1300. Tall narrow windows were typical.

**2 Decorated:** about 1300–1400. Spires were added and large wide windows with geometric patterns were typical.

**3 Perpendicular:** about 1400–1550. Very tall buildings. The wide windows had long vertical divisions running from top to bottom.

Interior of the restored church at Holy Cross, Co Tipperary. The window is in the Decorated style, but the walls are thick and typically Norman.

St Patrick's Church of Ireland Cathedral, Armagh. This is an 18th century restoration of a medieval building. It has a variety of styles. The large south window is Decorated but the five windows in the nave are Perpendicular.

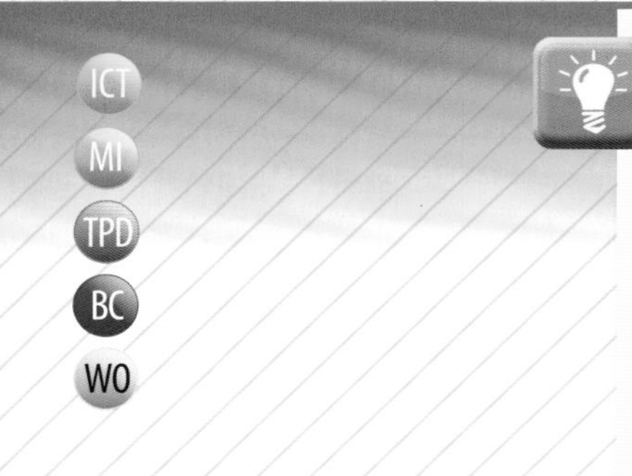


## PROJECT

In groups of three, find out more about each of the three styles of Gothic architecture. Each person should take one style and find at least one example of a church to illustrate it. Draw either a doorway or a window to illustrate each of the styles.

Make up a poster of information titled 'Gothic Architecture'. Try to make your poster at least A3 size (that's two A4 pages together). Make it bigger if you can.

Compose your poster carefully, with illustrations and text. Use appropriate language and a clear layout.

When all the posters are finished, put them up on the wall. Using post-it notes, under your poster, write down two things that you think you did well and one thing that you think you could have done better.

Then do the same for the posters of the other groups!

# UNIT 36: THE MONASTERY

## MONKS AND NUNS

When you read about the Early Middle Ages, you learned that Ireland already had dozens of monasteries long before the Normans came, but these did not have elaborate buildings like those in France. The purpose of a monastery was to provide a secluded place where those who wanted a religious life could cut themselves off from the distractions of the world and devote their time to prayer and the study of holy books. Men entered a **monastery** and women entered a **nunnery** (or convent).

Those entering the religious life took vows:

- Vow of obedience – to obey the abbot or abbess in charge.
- Vow of poverty – to give up all personal possessions.
- Vow of chastity – to have no sexual relations.

Men entering a monastery had the tops of their heads shaved to show they were devoting themselves to God. Nuns wore a wimple covering the head and neck. There were many different **orders** of monks, for example Benedictine, Carthusian and Dominican. Each had their own form of dress and their own rules.

## THE CISTERCIANS

The most important religious order in Ireland was the Cistercian Order. It was founded in France in 1098, and was brought to Ireland by St Malachy who founded Mellifont Abbey in Co Louth in 1142. The Cistercians followed reformed Benedictine rules, and believed in self-sufficiency. They grew all their own food and the lay brothers spent a lot of time farming. Cistercians kept sheep and even made their own habits (monk's clothing) out of sheep's wool. As their habits were wool-coloured they were called 'white monks'.

The Norman knight John de Courcy (see Unit 27) brought the Cistercians to Ulster. He founded Inch Abbey, near Downpatrick, in 1180, and his wife, Affreca, founded Grey Abbey, on the Ards Peninsula.

A Cistercian monk.

**LAY BROTHER:** a servant in a monastery.

## INCH ABBEY

### ACTIVITY

Look at these three images of Inch Abbey.

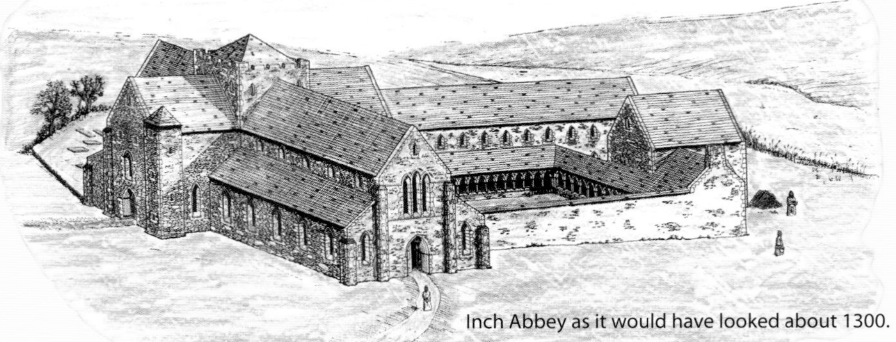

Inch Abbey as it would have looked about 1300.

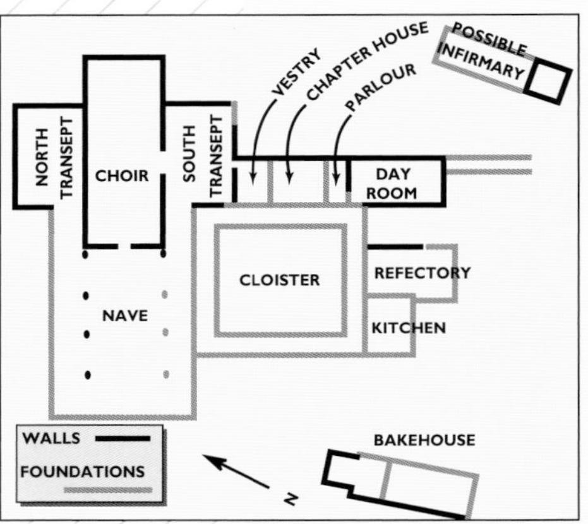


A diagram of Inch Abbey

The remains of Inch Abbey as they look today.

Compare these three illustrations. In each illustration, pick out (i) the north transept (ii) the south transept (iii) the area of the cloisters.

Although the size of each room varied, the layout of all Cistercian monasteries is the same. Study the diagram of Inch Abbey. Note the large cruciform (cross-shaped) church**,** facing roughly east.

Why do you think churches were made in a cruciform shape and why might they be built to face east?

On the south side is the **cloister** where the monks could relax or meditate. The eastern wing had the **vestry** (were the vestments and service equipment were kept); the **chapter house** (where a chapter of the rules was read every day); the **parlour** (where conversation was allowed); and a long **day room** (for indoor activities). Upstairs was the **dormitory** where the monks all slept. The monks ate in the **refectory,** which was in the southern wing along with the **kitchen.**

Nearby, Inch had another two buildings, one of which was probably an **infirmary** (hospital) and the other a **bakehouse** for baking bread.

What is the French word from which we get the English word 'parlour'?

## ACTIVITY

### Extended writing

You are a Cistercian monk who used to live and worship in Inch Abbey in 1300. You have travelled through time to visit the ruins today. You walk round the Abbey ruins. Later that night before you go to bed, you write a letter to another monk who was your friend when the Abbey was active. Tell him what you have done, what the Abbey looks like now, how you felt, what memories you recalled, and anything else that you think you might tell your friend. Try to use words and phrases that show your emotions.

## ACTIVITY

### Thought shower

In class, consider all the functions of a medieval monastery. What organisations carry out all these functions today? For example, instead of an infirmary, hospitals now look after the sick. After you have talked about this, discuss how important you think the monasteries were for medieval society.

## HOLY CROSS ABBEY

Holy Cross Abbey in Co Tipperary is the best preserved Irish medieval monastery. Like Inch, it was a Cistercian Abbey founded in the 12th century, but it was largely rebuilt and modernised in the 15th century with Decorated style windows and cloisters. For centuries the Abbey was a ruin. It was restored to its present state in the early 1970s. Using Holy Cross we can imagine life in a monastery very vividly.

Monks and nuns followed a very rigorous life in which their day was broken up by attendance at prayers. To make sure they did not fall asleep, the seats were hard and very narrow in the church. You can see seats like these in the picture of the cloisters at Holy Cross on the next page.

Even so, they did not always listen attentively, as this letter, from the Bishop of Winchester to the Abbess of Romsey, shows. It was written in 1387.

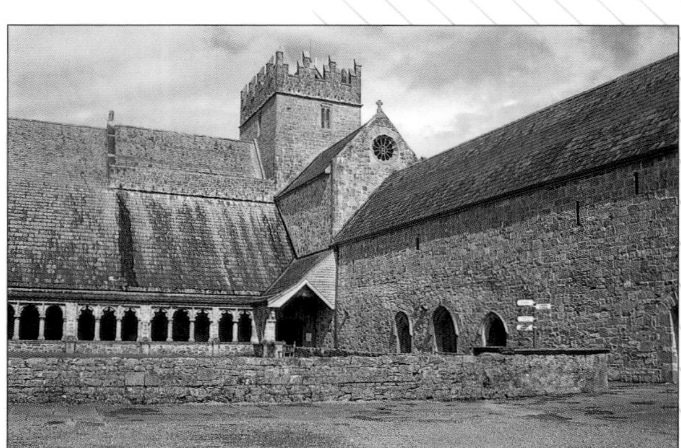

Holy Cross Abbey; the Abbey church and east range. The three doors (left to right) led to (1) the Chapter House; (2) a passage which led to the Abbot's house; (3) the parlour.

**RIGOROUS: Strict and needing a lot of energy**

> *We have convinced ourselves by clear proof that some nuns of your house bring with them to church birds, rabbits, hounds and such like things... and give more thought to them than to the services of the church... to the grievous peril of their souls.*

The cloisters. The green area was used for recreation such as bowls. The building besde the cloisters had cellars on the ground floor and a dormitory for the lay brothers.

Here is a typical day for a monk. Some services had their own Latin name.

| | |
|---|---|
| 2.00 am | Prayers. |
| 3.00 am | Back to bed. |
| 6.00 am | Prayers (Prime). |
| 6.30 am | Breakfast (bread and ale). |
| 7.00 am | Meeting in Chapter House. Monks who broke rules are disciplined. Tasks set for the day. Prayers. |
| 8.00 am | Lay brothers work in the fields or kitchen. Religious brothers walk in the cloisters, meditate or study. |
| 11.00 am | Prayers and communion. |
| Noon | Main meal, usually eaten in silence. |
| 12.30 pm | Prayers. |
| 1.00 pm | Lay brothers work in the fields. Religious brothers work in the gardens, fish, or relax. |
| 6.00 pm | Prayers (Vespers). |
| 7.00 pm | Supper. |
| 8.00 pm | Prayers (Compline). Retire to bed. |

1. How long is the longest period of unbroken sleep that the monks get?
2. How many times in the day did the monks attend prayers?
3. What might have attracted people to become monks or nuns (other than having a strong religious faith)?

## PILGRIMAGES

The most exciting religious event in the Middle Ages was to go on a **pilgrimage** to some very holy place. Canterbury in England became an important place of pilgrimage because it was where Archbishop Becket (St Thomas) was murdered.

In Ireland the most famous place of pilgrimage was Lough Derg in Co Donegal, where St Patrick's Island was believed to be the entrance to Purgatory (where, it was believed, people went after death). Holy Cross in Co Tipperary attracted pilgrims because it has a piece of wood believed to have come from Jesus' cross.

Pilgrims were given free food and shelter at monasteries and enjoyed a sort of holiday. They went for various reasons – as punishment for sins, to get a cure for the sick, or simply as an excuse to leave the village. Pilgrims collected small cap badges from shrines they had visited, to prove they had been.

Why do you think pilgrimages were regarded as so exciting?

# REVIEW THIS SECTION

## Review your work

In Unit 14 you were asked to make notes on what you thought you knew about the Normans. Take your notes out again and look over what you said.

How many things did you get right?

Were you very wrong about some things?

Was there anything about the Normans that surprised you?

Is there anything more you would like to know? If so, have a discussion in class to see if anyone knows the answer.

## ACTIVITY

**Extended writing**

A lot happened in the High Middle Ages! That is why this Section is so long.

1. Have a look back over all the Units in this Section and make notes about anything that particularly interested you.

   Then write about three of those events. Give your own opinion on what happened. Your teacher will tell you how much to write.

2. Write half a page titled *either* (i) Why I would like to live in the High Middle Ages *or* (ii) Why I would not like to live in the High Middle Ages. (Would it depend on who you were?)

## ACTIVITY

**Your timeline**

Draw a timeline and mark on it all the dates that you have read about in this section and what happened on those dates.

## Word Check

Check out these words to make sure you can spell them.

| | | |
|---|---|---|
| **anchorite** | **military** | **Canute** |
| **Conqueror** | **Westminster** | **scholar** |
| **Domesday** | **category** | **Pevensey** |
| **rebellion** | **sceptre** | **counsellor** |
| **Thames** | **Stamford** | **judgement** |
| **quotation** | **Bayeux** | **exhausted** |
| **invasion** | **Atheling** | |

If you're not sure if you can spell any of them, check them out a few more times.

# END OF SECTION QUIZ

## Class Quiz!

Divide into two teams and decide on a prize for the winning team. If you get a question right, your team gets a point, BUT if you get a question wrong, you lose a point! So think carefully before you answer.

1. Where did William land in England in 1066?
2. What is a lay brother?
3. Who lived in a street called The Shambles?
4. Name the castle in Co Antrim built by John de Courcy.
5. What was the date of the Harrying of the North?
6. Who hid in the Isle of Ely?
7. In what county is Holy Cross Abbey?
8. Where is the Stone of Scone kept?
9. What was a 'masterpiece'?
10. Who founded Westminster Abbey?
11. William the Conqueror ordered the writing of the Anglo-Saxon Chronicles. True or false?
12. What is an anchorite?
13. Name two of the contenders for the throne after the death of Edward the Confessor.
14. What was The Domesday Book?
15. Where is the White Tower?
16. In a monastery, what was the infirmary?
17. Name a famous place of pilgrimage in Ireland.
18. After what battle was Brian Boru killed?
19. The Battle of Stamford Bridge was fought between which two sides?
20. Name two writers who wrote about the events of the High Middle Ages.

# THE LATE MIDDLE AGES
# UNIT 37: THE BLACK DEATH

In this final section you will be studying the Late Middle Ages. You will be learning about an important writer of the time called Geoffrey Chaucer. Chaucer wrote fictional accounts of people of his time. Have a discussion in class about the value of fiction to an historian. Can fiction contribute anything to the understanding of a time period?

**FICTION: novels, stories that are made up and didn't really happen.**

## A TERRIBLE PLAGUE

In 1348 a terrible plague called the **Black Death** reached England. It had been travelling across Europe from Asia along the world's trade routes.

The plague was a killer, and medieval doctors had no idea what caused it. If you caught it you came out in black spots. Sores developed and then burst. You died in agony, usually within five days. If you caught the plague, you had only a 10% chance of surviving. Within three years it had killed a third of the population of Europe. In 1349 it reached Ireland.

Here are two contemporary accounts of the effects of the plague:

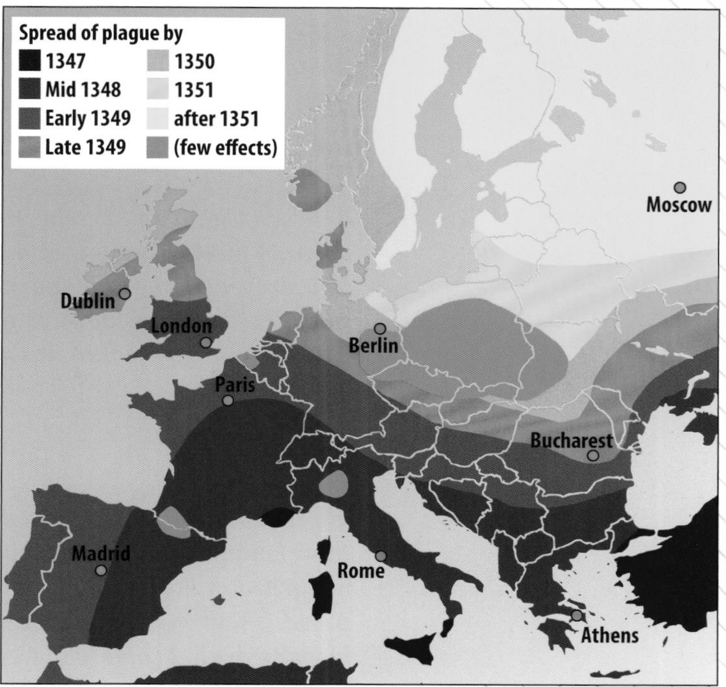


Map showing how the plague spread across Europe from 1347 to 1351. The boundaries of modern countries are shown.

> *In men and women alike it first showed itself in the groin or armpits. Some grew as large as an apple or an egg. From these two parts of the body this deadly swelling soon began to spread in all directions. Then black spots began to appear on the arms or thigh.*

From the introduction to *The Decameron* by Boccaccio, 1351

> *This pestilence was so contagious that those who touched the dead or persons sick with the plague were straightaway infected themselves and died. Many died from boils and ulcers and running sores which grew on the legs and beneath the armpits while others suffered pains in the head and went almost into a frenzy, whilst others spat blood.*

Written by a Franciscan monk, Kilkenny, Ireland

The boils that developed on the bodies of infected people were called 'buboes'. These give the other common name of the disease: **bubonic plague**.

# ORIGINS

People at the time did not know what caused the plague. Here are three different accounts from the time, each of which tries to explain its origin:

> *In the east, in a place near India, there were horrors and storms for three days. On the first day out of the sky there fell frogs, snakes, lizards, scorpions and other poisonous animals. On the second day there was thunder and lightening: sheets of fire and stinking smoke came from heaven: this filled all the remaining men and animals and destroyed all the towns. These storms infected the whole place, then a southern wind spread the infection to the whole sea shore and the surrounding places. The plague is getting worse every day.*

A monk living in Flanders (in modern Belgium) in 1346

> *Between China and Persia [Iran] a vast rain of fire fell, coming down in flakes like snow and burning up the mountains and plain. It destroyed all the land and all the people. Then huge amounts of smoke rose up: anyone looking at this died in less than twelve hours. Also anyone who looked at someone who had seen the smoke also quickly died.*

*Chronicle of Este*, around 1346

> *Throughout the years 1348 and 1349 huge numbers of people died, both men and women and the young more than the old. This happened in Paris and all through France, and in other parts of the world. There were so many corpses that it was almost impossible to bury them all. People who were completely healthy became ill for only two or three days and then they died. Someone who was well one day might be dead the next and carried to his grave. Swellings appeared suddenly under the armpits or in the groin – these were certain signs that the people would die. This sickness or plague was called an epidemic by the doctors. Nothing like it has been heard of or seen in recent times. The reason the disease is spread is because of contagion: if a healthy person visited a plague victim, he usually died himself. This in fact frightened some of the priests in the town and they fled. They left the care of the sick to other priests who had more courage.*

Jean de Venette, a French monk living in Paris

Other people thought the plague was caused by:

- Jews or nobles poisoning the drinking water.
- God, as a punishment for sin.
- The devil.
- Poison vapours from an earthquake in northern Italy in 1348.
- The close position of Saturn, Jupiter and Mars in 1345.

## ACTIVITY

Make a list of what people of the time thought caused the plague.
What do you think the first two sources are describing?
How useful are the three sources from the time of the plague, to the historian?

## CURES

Here are some of the cures that people at the time tried:

- Shutting themselves away from everyone and drinking only milk or wine.
- Flogging themselves to show they were sorry for their sins.
- Leaving the towns and fleeing to the countryside.
- Cover their mouths with a mask or carrying herbs.
- Carrying on as normal and hoping for the best.

Other cures were tried, many of which seem very odd to us. Here is one:

> *Take a live frog and lay the belly of it next to the plague sore; if the patient will escape, the frog will burst in a quarter of an hour; then lay on another; and this you do till no more burst, for they draw forth the poison. If none of the frogs do burst, the person will not escape.*

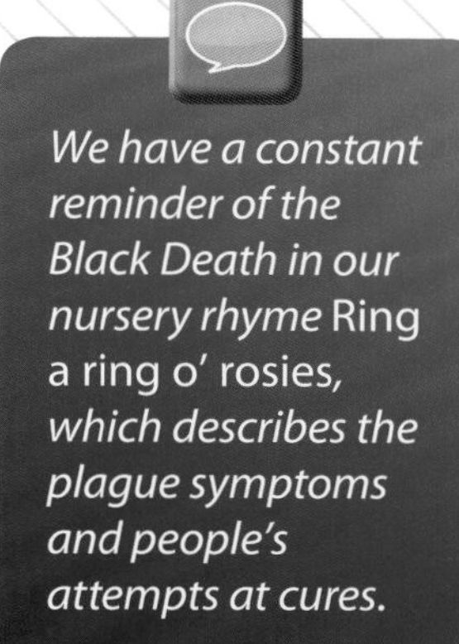


### THE FLAGELLANTS

The **flagellants** were people who felt that God was punishing them by sending the plague. They walked about beating themselves in order to show repentance. Here is a contemporary description of these people:

> *They gathered together in large groups and marched in procession with their backs bare. When they got to crossroads, or the market squares of towns, they formed circles and beat their bare backs with weighted whips... The flagellants lashed at their shoulders and arms with whips which had iron points at the end. They whipped themselves so hard they drew blood...*

Flagellants beating each other at Doornik in 1349. From *The Chronicle of Aegidus Li Muisis* (14th century).

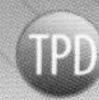


1. What does the word 'flagellant' mean?
2. In many areas, cases of plague rose in towns where the flagellants had passed. Why would that be?

## WHAT REALLY CAUSED THE PLAGUE?

The plague was caused by a germ, which was identified in 1894. It was carried by fleas that live on black rats. If the flea bit a human, the human caught the plague. The flea is called *xenopsylla cheopis*.

Because they lacked this important medical knowledge, many things the people did actually helped the disease to spread instead of attacking it. For example, some thought that the plague had been sent by the devil. Cats were thought to be friends of the devil so cats were killed in their thousands. Of course, cats kill rats and since we now know that it was rats that were carrying the infected fleas, this actually helped to spread the plague.

1. If the real cause of the plague had been known in 1348, how could people have reduced their chances of catching it?
2. Do you think the poor were any more likely to catch the plague than the rich? Why or why not?
3. What does the reaction of the population to the Black Death tell us about the beliefs of the people of the time?

## EFFECTS OF THE PLAGUE

The plague arrived in Ireland through the port of Howth (near Dublin) in July 1348. In Ireland, unlike Britain, ports and towns were the places most badly affected by the disease. This may be because the Irish lived in more isolated areas in the country and were less likely to come into contact with it. Because of this, although many Irish died, it was the Anglo-Norman colonies in Ireland that were struck hardest.

Across Europe millions of people died. These tables show the size of the population of England before and after the plague:

| Year | Population |
|---|---|
| 1050 | 1,500,000 |
| 1080 | 2,000,000 |
| 1100 | 2,200,000 |
| 1150 | 2,800,000 |

| Year | Population |
|---|---|
| 1200 | 3,500,000 |
| 1250 | 4,000,000 |
| 1300 | 4,700,000 |
| 1348 | 5,200,000 |

| Year | Population |
|---|---|
| 1375 | 2,800,000 |
| 1400 | 2,600,000 |
| 1450 | 2,200,000 |
| 1500 | 2,600,000 |

| Year | Population |
|---|---|
| 1530 | 2,800,000 |
| 1550 | 3,100,000 |
| 1600 | 4,000,000 |
| 1700 | 5,700,000 |

## ACTIVITY

Use the figures in the table to draw a line graph of the population of England from 1050 to 1700.

1. By how much did the population fall between 1348 and 1375?
2. Why do you think this was?
3. When did the population return to the level it had been in 1348 (before the plague)?
4. How many years did it take for the population to recover and reach the 1348 level again?

The main effects of the Black Death were:

- Huge loss of life, and a major fall in population across Europe.
- The appearance of the Flagellants.
- People became obsessed with death.
- Many peasants died and complete villages were abandoned.
- The lords of the manors found there was a shortage of peasants to work their land.
- The peasants realised this and demanded higher wages. Wages rose by up to 50%.
- The church lost some of its influence over people because it was obvious that the clergy could not affect the course of the disease and indeed they died just the same as everyone else.

A grave slab in Drogheda made at the time of the Black Death in Ireland, showing people's obsession with death.

## ACTIVITY

The population of the country nearly halved. This had a great effect on the lives of the people who remained. Remember that the economy was overwhelmingly based on agriculture and on growing your own food.

Write a paragraph on each of the following, saying how you think the Black Death affected it.

**The land**

**Taxes**

**Medicine**

**The nobility (lords)**

**Food**

**Monasteries who cared for the sick**

**The church**

**Villages**

# UNIT 38: THE PEASANTS' REVOLT

## CAUSES

Richard II

In 1377 Richard II became king at the age of ten. He introduced a new tax called the **Poll Tax.** In 1380 the Poll Tax was trebled. Many peasants avoided paying by hiding or telling lies about the number of people in their family. In March 1381 King Richard ordered the arrest of anyone who refused to pay the Poll Tax. A priest named **John Ball** was one of those imprisoned. The **Peasants' Revolt** that followed later in 1381 was the most serious event of its kind in the Middle Ages.

What age was Richard II at the time of the Peasants' Revolt?

There were four main causes of the Peasants' Revolt:

- **The Black Death:** Peasants who had lived through and survived the Black Death felt they were special: God had protected them. Because there were fewer labourers for the lords' lands, the peasants demanded higher wages and were able to improve their lifestyles.
- **Wages:** there was discontent among the peasants because Parliament in 1351 had passed the **Statute of Labourers**. This stopped them from being paid higher wages than they got in 1347 (before the Black Death).
- **Agitation:** Preachers such as John Ball, a priest in Kent, and peasant leaders like **Wat Tyler** stirred up the people by saying that all men should be equal and that the poor should not pay taxes.
- **Taxes:** Richard II introduced the Poll Tax in 1377 to pay for a war in France. This was the first time that peasants, not just the nobility, had been taxed. 'Poll' means 'head', and it was called this because everyone over 15 had to pay. In 1377 and 1378 they paid 4d (old pennies, about 2p now), but in 1380 this was increased 12d (about 5p).

John Ball

## JOHN BALL

Here is part of a speech by John Ball:

> *Good people, all is not well in England, nor will they be until everyone is equal and there are neither villeins nor gentlemen, and Lords are no greater than we are... They are dressed in velvet, while we have to wear poor cloth. They have fine houses while we have to work in the wind and rain of the fields. Let us go to the king, he is young, and show him what slavery we are in. Let us tell him that we want things to be put right or else we will do something about it ourselves.*

From John Ball's sermon at Blackheath, quoted by Jean Froissart, *Chronicles*, about 1390

This is what some other writers of the day said about John Ball:

> *John Ball taught the people that tithes ought not to be paid... He also taught the perverse doctrines of John Wycliffe.*

John Walsingham's *A History of England*, written around 1395. (John Wycliffe argued for reforms based on Biblical principles, and a reduction in the power of the church.)

> *John Ball has several times been confined in the Archbishop of Canterbury's prison for his absurd speeches. For it was his habit on Sundays after mass, when everyone was coming out of Church, to collect a crowd around him in the market place and address them... and in their envy of the rich the peasants began to murmur... that the country was badly governed.*

Jean Froissart, *Chronicles*

> *At this time the commons had as their leader a chaplain of evil disposition named John Ball, who advised them to get rid of all the lords and archbishops.*

*Chronicle of St Mary's*, York, around 1380

## ACTIVITY

1. Do the other writers agree with John Ball? Give evidence to support your conclusion.
2. What would each of these people have thought of John Ball's sermon:
   (a) the peasants who heard him (b) the lords in London (c) King Richard II?
3. Do you think John Ball is issuing a threat in his speech? What makes you think this?
4. Conduct an interview with John Ball. Pick one person to sit at the front of the class as John Ball and put questions to him about his ideas for reforming society in the Late Middle Ages.

# THE REVOLT BEGINS

In May 1381, a tax collector, Thomas Bampton arrived at the Essex village of Fobbing to find out why the people there had not paid their Poll Tax. The villagers threw him out. In June, soldiers arrived to establish law and order. They too were thrown out, because the villagers of Fobbing had organised themselves, and many other local villages in Essex had joined them in their stand against the tax. The villagers decided to march on London to plead with the young King to listen to their complaints.

## ACTIVITY

This was a popular rhyme of the rebels:

"When Adam delved and Eve span
Who was then the Gentleman?"

*'Delved' here means 'dug'. 'Span' means 'spun'.*

Work out what this rhyme means. The clue is the cause they were fighting for.

## ACTIVITY

Imagine the peasants were able to use modern materials and methods of protest. Make some protest banners and placards that they might have carried. Remember they will need to be easily read and brief. Make the words memorable, like the modern 'One man, one vote!' slogan. How could they use Internet-based social media to get their message across? You could march round the classroom as if you were the rebels marching on London!

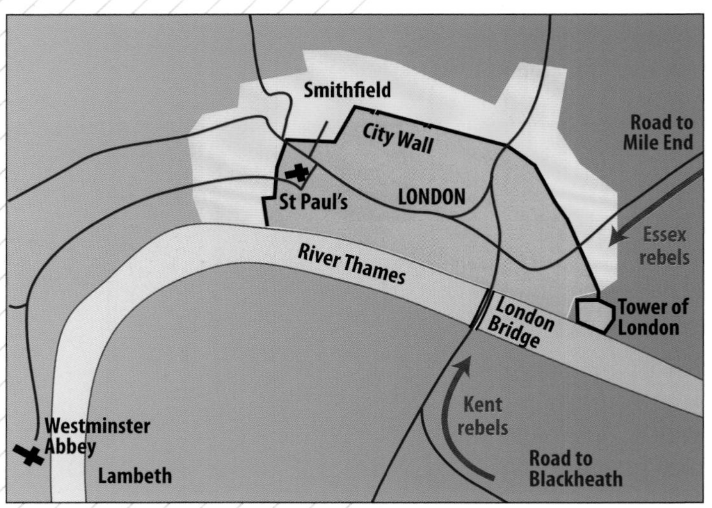


Map of London in 1381 showing how the rebels approached the capital.

## TIMELINE OF THE REVOLT

**May:** Commissioners are sent by the king to find the tax dodgers. Riots break out in Essex and Kent. Some tax collectors are murdered.

**June 6:** Peasants from Kent capture Rochester Castle. They march to Maidstone and release John Ball who had been imprisoned again. Wat Tyler is chosen as their leader.

**June 10:** Led by Wat Tyler, peasants go to Canterbury and destroy the palace of **Simon Sudbury**, the Archbishop of Canterbury. Sudbury had introduced the Poll Tax.

**June 11:** Peasants from Essex and Kent march to London.

**June 12:** The Essex rebels camp at Mile End, near London. The Kent rebels camp at Blackheath. Richard II and the government take refuge in the Tower of London.

**June 13:** John Ball preaches to the rebels at Blackheath. The king tries to speak to them from a boat in the Thames, then returns to the Tower. The rebels enter London and behead several royal officials. Palaces are burnt.

**June 14:** Richard II, the Mayor and some lords meet the rebels at Mile End. Wat Tyler states his demands:

- freedom for all men
- abolition of all labour service to lords
- fair wages for everyone
- no more Poll Taxes
- a free pardon for everyone who had come to London
- punishment for the king's 'evil advisors'

While the king is at Mile End, Kent rebels enter the Tower and execute four advisors, including Sudbury. Riots in London.

**June 15:** The King, with 200 followers, meets the rebels at Smithfield. Tyler makes more demands and speaks rudely to the King. He is attacked and killed. The peasants draw their bows and are about to shoot when Richard II says "Sirs, will ye shoot your king? I will be your Captain. Follow me". He leads them out of London. The King gives out charters agreeing to Tyler's demands and the peasants go home contented.

A picture painted about 1460 showing the events of June 15. On the left Wat Tyler is attacked, and on the right Richard II faces the peasants.

## RESULTS OF THE REVOLT

A week later the King went back on his promises. He arrested all the rebel leaders and executed them. The charters were torn up. The King said "Peasants you are and peasants you will remain". A wave of terror followed in the villages of Kent and Essex. John Ball was hanged, drawn and quartered on 15 July, 1381.

The revolt really frightened the government. The King never again tried to collect Poll Tax. Parliament still tried to keep wages down, but after a few years it gave up. Gradually over the next 100 years the system of labour service on manors was abandoned. It was the beginning of the end of feudalism in England.

Why do you think the revolt failed? Try to pick out the event that was the turning point for the rebels.

## RESEARCH

John Ball was an interesting person.

Research his life and write his obituary for a newspaper.

When you had learned more about John Ball, did you feel sympathetic or unsympathetic to him? Explain how you came to your conclusion.

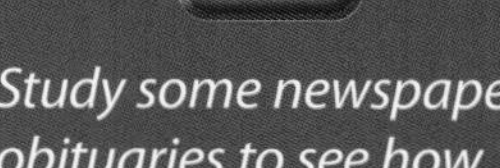

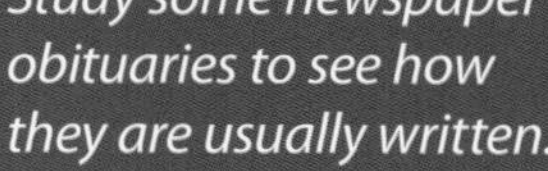

*Study some newspaper obituaries to see how they are usually written.*

## ACTIVITY

Choose an issue from today's world that you feel strongly about. Plan a protest to highlight the issue. What would you do? How would you do it? How would you make sure that as many people as possible heard about the issue? What methods and tools would you use?

*The Peasants' Revolt* involved many people. How many peasants would have been involved if the rebellion had been known as *The Peasant's Revolt?* (Look where the apostrophe is.)

# UNIT 39: GEOFFREY CHAUCER

## CHAUCER'S LIFE

Geoffrey Chaucer (pronounced 'Chawser') is one of the most famous of all poets writing in English. He was born about 1340 in London. His father was a wine merchant and his family was quite wealthy. In 1357, Chaucer became a page (servant) to Elizabeth, the Countess of Ulster, who was the wife of one of Edward III's sons.

Edward III invaded France in 1359 and Chaucer went with him as part of the army. The next year, Chaucer was captured by the French and imprisoned. The king paid a ransom of £16 to have him released. That would be nearly £6000 in today's money.

He went on to have a very eventful career in public life as a courtier to Edward III and Richard II.

Chaucer lived through the violent times of the Peasants' Revolt (see Unit 38). In fact he knew many of those who were executed. He left London for Kent in order to escape the turmoil and in 1386 he became a Member of Parliament for the county. He died in 1400.

Geoffrey Chaucer is sometimes called **The Father of English Literature.** This is because he wrote poetry in English. This might not seem strange to us, but at the time Chaucer was living, nearly all literature was written in Latin or French. The everyday language was Middle English and this wasn't thought to be good enough for poetry and other forms of literature. However, because Chaucer wrote in English, other writers began to do the same and so we have a rich legacy of English literature starting from this time. (In the later 16th century, William Shakespeare composed some of the most beautiful English ever written when he wrote his plays.)

## THE CANTERBURY TALES

Chaucer's most famous poem is *The Canterbury Tales*. This is a long composition about a group of people going on a pilgrimage from Southwark in London to Canterbury Cathedral. Along the way, the pilgrims have a story-telling contest and each one tells a tale. The work is divided into, for example, *The Pardoner's Tale, The Monk's Tale, The Wife of Bath's Tale* and *The Priest's Tale.*

Wood engravings of The Knight and The Prioress, two of the Canterbury pilgrims.

Chaucer started the Tales with an introductory section called *The Prologue*. Here is part of it, with a translation alongside:

| | |
|---|---|
| *Bifil that in that seson on a day,* | *Befell that, in that season, on a day* |
| *In southwerk at the tabard as I lay* | *In Southwark, at the Tabard, as I lay* |
| *Redy to wenden on my pilgrymage* | *Ready to start upon my pilgrimage* |
| *To caunterbury with ful devout corage,* | *To Canterbury, full of devout homage,* |
| *At nyght was come into that hostelrye* | *There came at nightfall to that hostelry* |
| *Wel nyne and twenty in a compaignye,* | *Some nine and twenty in a company* |
| *Of sondry folk, by aventure yfalle* | *Of sundry persons who had chanced to fall* |
| *In felaweshipe, and pilgrimes were they alle,* | *In fellowship, and pilgrims were they all* |
| *That toward caunterbury wolden ryde.* | *That toward Canterbury town would ride.* |

# ACTIVITY

## Class discussion

*The Canterbury Tales* are stories about the lives, experiences and opinions of a group of very different people living in the 14th century. Discuss the advantages to an historian of studying them.

# RESEARCH

ICT

Design a tourist brochure for pilgrims going to Canterbury at the time of Chaucer. Why would they want to go? What would they see? Where would they stay?

# ACTIVITY

Write a poem called *The Pupil's Tale*.
Perhaps some of these poems could be read in class and put up on display.

THE LATE MIDDLE AGES

# UNIT 40: THE NORMAN LEGACY

During the period covered by this book, life had changed a great deal for people in England, Scotland, Wales and Ireland. Many new things had been invented, eg the spinning wheel, guns and gunpowder. The first **windmills** had appeared about the time of the Battle of Hastings. Between 1350 and 1390 the first public clocks appeared in churches. In 1477 **William Caxton** started the first **printing press** in England. European explorers had sailed by sea to Africa, India and China. In 1492 **Columbus discovered America.** Much more was known about the world than was known in 1066.

Today we can still see a lot of things which have survived from the Middle Ages, and which are part of the legacy which has been left to us by the Normans. Here are some of the permanent effects which the Normans and their successors have left in Ireland:

**Language:** One of the official languages of the Republic of Ireland is Irish, a language loved by many people. But most people in Ireland, north and south, use English as their everyday language. English was brought to Ireland by the Normans and has remained ever since.

**Castles:** All over Ireland there are castles, some still lived in and used, but most ruined. There are over 2000 castles in Ireland and most of them were built in the Middle Ages. In many parts of Ulster, like Clough, Co Down, we can see the remains of the Norman motte and bailey castles.

**Towns:** Before the Normans there were no towns in Ireland apart from the Viking settlements like Dublin. Many towns founded by the Normans, such as Carrickfergus, Ardglass and Carlingford, still exist today.

**Law and government:** The Normans and their successors began to replace the ancient system of Irish law with English Common Law. Our laws today are based on this law. The Normans were the first to introduce parliaments to Ireland, and the first to begin to divide Ireland into counties.

**Churches:** The modern Roman Catholic Church in Ireland is the legacy of the changes to the organisation of the church introduced by the Normans in the Middle Ages. More visible signs of the Normans are the ruined monasteries and abbeys found in many parts of Ireland.

**Surnames:** Many of the family names of Ireland today have Norman origins. A number of names begin with 'Fitz'. This means 'son of'. Fitzstephen means 'son of Stephen'. Here are some Norman names still common today: Burke, Butler, Costello, Fitzgerald, Fitzmaurice, Power, Roche, Walsh, Savage.

A Norman surname still evident in Carlingford, county Louth today.

**Q** What aspects of the Norman legacy do you think we should work to preserve? Explain your answer. What careers today involve preserving the Norman legacy?

# END OF SECTION QUIZ

## Class Quiz!

Divide into two teams and decide on a prize for the winning team. If you get a question right, your team gets a point, BUT if you get a question wrong, you lose a point! So think carefully before you answer.

1. What age was Richard II when he became king?
2. Where did the pilgrims described in *The Canterbury Tales* start their journey from?
3. Name two possible 14th century cures for the Black Death.
4. In what country was Chaucer imprisoned?
5. Who said "Peasants you are and peasants you will remain"?
6. Through what port did the Black Death enter Ireland?
7. How much money did the king pay as a ransom for Chaucer when he was imprisoned?
8. Name one of the tales from The Canterbury Tales.
9. "The native Irish were struck worst by the Black Death." True or false?
10. What is a word for stories that are made up, such as novels?
11. Why did people kill cats during the Black Death?
12. Who was John Ball?
13. Why did the peasants demand higher wages after the Black Death?
14. What were your chances of surviving if you caught the Plague?
15. Finish this rhyme: "When Adam delved and Eve span …"

## Word Check

Check out these words to make sure you can spell them.

**fiction**
**Canterbury**
**population**
**labourer**
**pilgrimage**
**plague**
**contagious**
**interview**
**placard**
**cathedral**
**knight**
**pestilence**
**Cistercian**
**archbishop**
**prologue**
**literature**
**courtier**
**wealthy**
**bubonic**
**abolition**

If you're not sure if you can spell any of them, check them out a few more times.

## ACTIVITY

**Your timeline**

Create a timeline of all the events you have learnt about in the Late Middle Ages. Pick one event or one person that particularly interested you and write a paragraph giving your reasons for your choice.

THE MEDIEVAL WORLD

# CONCLUSION

## ACTIVITY

Now that you have finished your study of the Middle Ages, share in class all your impressions of the period. For example:

Was it a good or a bad time to be alive?

What adjectives would you use to describe the Middle Ages?

Do you think it is correct to call them The Dark Ages?

So many things have changed over the centuries since then. Is there anything that you wish had survived into our time?

# MEDIEVAL KINGS OF ENGLAND

| | |
|---|---|
| **871–899** | Alfred the Great (first King of all England) |
| **899–924** | Edward the Elder (son of Alfred the Great) |
| **924–939** | Athelstan (son of Edward the Elder) |
| **939–946** | Edmund I (son of Edward the Elder) |
| **946–955** | Edred (son of Edward the Elder) |
| **955–959** | Eadwig (son of Edward the Elder) |
| **959–975** | Edgar the Peaceful (son of Edmund I) |
| **975–978** | Edward the Martyr (son of Edgar) |
| **978–1013** | Ethelred the Unready (son of Edgar) |
| **1013–1014** | Sweyn I (of Denmark) |
| **1014–1016** | Ethelred the Unready (son of Edgar) |
| **1016–1035** | Canute (of Denmark) (son of Sweyn I) |
| **1035–1040** | Harold I (the Harefoot) (son of Canute) |
| **1040–1042** | Hardicanute (son of Canute) |
| **1042–1066** | Edward the Confessor |
| **1066** | Harold II |
| **1066–1087** | King William I (William the Conqueror) |
| **1087–1100** | King William II (William Rufus, son of William the Conqueror) |
| **1100–1135** | King Henry I (brother of William Rufus) |
| **1135–1154** | King Stephen (nephew of Henry I) |
| **1154–1189** | King Henry II (grandson of Henry I) |
| **1189–1199** | King Richard I (third son of Henry II) |
| **1199–1216** | King John (fifth son of Henry II) |
| **1216–1272** | King Henry III (son of John) |
| **1272–1307** | King Edward I (son of Henry III) |
| **1307–1327** | King Edward II (son of Edward I) |
| **1327–1377** | King Edward III (son of Edward II) |
| **1377–1399** | King Richard II (grandson of Edward III, son of the Black Prince) |
| **1399–1413** | King Henry IV (grandson of Edward III, son of John of Gaunt) |
| **1413–1422** | King Henry V (son of Henry IV) |
| **1422–1461** | King Henry VI (son of Henry V) |
| **1461–1483** | King Edward IV (youngest son of Edward III ) |
| **1483–1485** | King Richard III (uncle of Edward V) |

# COPYRIGHT NOTICES

*The following images are licensed under the Creative Commons Attribution 2.0, 2.5 and 3.0 Licenses. Permission is granted to share and/or remix this work providing the work is attributed in the manner specified by the author or licensor. Copies of these licenses can be viewed at:*
*http://creativecommons.org/licenses/by/2.0/deed.en*
*http://creativecommons.org/licenses/by/2.5/*
*http://creativecommons.org/licenses/by/3.0/*
19 upper (Phil Price), lower (Brian Lincolnian), 30 wheat (3268zauber), 31 cows (Mellissa McCloud), sheep (Kevin McManus), pig (Amanda Slater), chicken (Ernst Vikne), beehive (Carly Lesser & Art Drauglis), 32, 33 upper (Dr Steven Plunkett), 34 lyre, belt buckle, reconstructed helmet, 46 upper (Jacob Rus), 49 (Michael Shea), 55 and 57 Westminster Abbey (Joshua Albers), 96 (ChrisO).

*The following images are licensed under the GNU Free Documentation License. Permission is granted to copy, distribute and/or modify this document under the terms of the GNU Free Documentation License, Version 1.2 or any later version published by the Free Software Foundation; with Invariant Sections, no Front-Cover Texts, and no Back-Cover Texts. A copy of this license can be viewed at:*
*http://www.gnu.org/licenses/fdl.html*
28 upper (Hans Musil), 30 rye (LSDSL) 74 (Bernard Gagnon).

*iStockphoto:* 26, 31 (goat, ploughing), 46 (lower), 57 (upper), 72, 96 (lower), 122, 128 (both lower)

*By kind permission of the City of Bayeux:* 53–55, 59, 66, 68, 101, 103

*John Brogan:* 29

*Down County Museum, Downpatrick:* 28, 85 (lower)

*Geraldine Tralee Exhibition, Tralee, Co Kerry:* 105 (upper), 107 (lower), 108

*Audrey M Hodge:* 107 (upper)

*Norman Johnston:* 40 (both), 63, 82, 84, 85 (top), 90 (lower), 95, 97 (all), 98 (all), 104 (upper), 105 (lower), 106, 110, 111 (both), 114 (photo), 115, 116 (both), 123, 130

*Sheila Johnston:* 64 (both)

*Mansell Collection:* 121

*What Really Happened? Did Canute Get His Feet Wet? by Nicolle, Pat (Patrick) (1907-95) Private Collection/ © Look and Learn/ The Bridgeman Art Library:* 37

*National Gallery of Ireland:* 24

*© Crown Copyright reproduced with the permission of the Controller of Her Majesty's Stationery Office:* 90 (upper), 92 (both), 93, 94, 114 (top), 135

*The photographs of scenes inside Carrickfergus Castle were taken with the kind co-operation of the Department for the Environment for Northern Ireland (Historic Monuments and Buildings Branch).*

*The photographs taken inside the Ulster History Park were taken with the kind permission of Omagh District Council.*

COLOURPOINT
EDUCATIONAL